SUCCESS
Is All In Your Head

**How to
Create Success
and
Love Your Life**

by
Angele Charbonneau

1 How to reprogram your thought processes to expect – and consistently find – success.

2 How your subconscious mind controls whether or not you achieve goals and make more money.

3 How to manage and overcome obstacles, detours, and objections.

SUCCESS
Is All In Your Head

How to Create Success
and Love Your Life

Copyright © 2012
by Angele Charbonneau

ISBN-13: 978-1480162822
ISBN-10: 1480162825

All rights reserved. No part of this book may be reproduced or transmitted in any form or by any means without written permission from the author.

Acknowledgements and Dedication

No one walks alone on the journey of life and success. I have been blessed to know many great people who encouraged me to write this book in order to share my insights on the secrets to maintaining a positive approach to life despite what it throws your way and helping others understand that success is for everyone! There are so many people who have joined me, walked beside me, and continuously helped me; I thank you all!

The concepts in this book are based largely on the broad teachings of others, compiled in a way that I believe has created great success in my life and will do the same for you. It is my hope that this book will honor the many who have made it possible through their pioneering research, insights and creativity.

Much of what I have learned over the years is the result of being a mother to five wonderful, delightful children: Zacharie, Tristan, Cassandre, Xavier and Charlize. All of them, in their own ways, inspired me and subconsciously made a tremendous contribution to the content of this book. A little bit of each of them will be found here weaving in and out of the pages! They have been the biggest "why" in my life! Thank you for being so understanding when mommy wasn't always able to be there. Everything I did, I did for you!

I also have to thank T. Harv Eker, who has taught me so many principles through attending his many incredible seminars on wealth and personal development. Over the years, he and the many speakers who have shared the same stage have taught me much about myself and the mysterious ways of life. They have taught me that success is simply a decision one must make, encouraging me to just go and do it! I can never thank you enough!

I also want to thank a wonderful man whose teachings were paramount to my success, and that is Blair Singer. He taught me to master the voice inside my head that continuously wants to take me out of the game. Thank you, Blair, for your wisdom, kindness and knowledge.

I also want to thank Sam Crowley, my coach and mentor, and Candace Morehouse, who were the catalysts in pushing and helping me to complete this book. I cannot thank you enough for your encouragement and your coaching. Writing a book has been a dream of mine for over twenty years. Thank you for making this dream come true and allowing me to share what burns at the very core of my being so that I may help others!

I'd like to thank my parents, my siblings, and my husband's family, especially my mother-in-law, who has passed away. They have always supported me throughout my career and helped in any way possible. They have always encouraged me and believed in me. Each one of you is near and dear to my heart! I am grateful for your patience while I continued to take on challenges that took time I could have spent with you. I love you all!

To all my staff: thank you so much for believing in all my quirky ways of teaching and training. You are like family to me. Thank you for trusting that the system works!! It was because of you that I wanted to write this book and share this knowledge with so many.

I would like to thank Jim Rohn, Tom Hopkins, Wayne Dyer, Brian Tracy, Tony Robbins, and Robert Kiyosaki for sharing so much of their wisdom and knowledge. Their understanding of human nature, ideas for life, and tips for success all contributed to the completion of this book. Thanks, guys. You are a true inspiration.

Thanks to all my friends, for sharing my happiness when starting this project and following with encouragement when it seemed too difficult to complete. I would have probably given up without your love and support.

Most of all, I would like to thank my husband and life partner, Michael, for standing beside me throughout my career and through the writing of this book. He has been my inspiration and motivation for continuing to learn all I can and move my career forward. He is my rock, and the reason I continuously strive to do better. I dedicate this book to him.

Contents

Acknowledgements and Dedication i

Foreword. xi

Introduction. 3

Chapter 1: Getting Your Mind Onboard
With Your Goals 19

    EXERCISE: Reprogramming
    Self-Limiting Beliefs 36

Chapter 2: Steer Your Mind Toward Success 43

    Exercise 1: Replace the Negative
    with a Positive. 64

    Exercise 2: Creative Visualization 65

Chapter 3: Thinking Past Your Comfort Zone . . . 69

    Exercise 1: Working Past Anxiety 83

    Exercise 2: Exploring Your CZ Boundaries . . 85

Chapter 4: Get the Car Out of the Garage. 89

    Exercise: Standing Up to Naysayers. 122

Chapter 5: That Voice in Your Head is
Giving You the Wrong Directions. 125

Exercise: Boast About Yourself 152

Chapter 6: Decide on Success with the
Power of Intention. 155

Exercise: 8 Steps for Harnessing the
Power of Intention to Achieve Goals 172

Chapter 7: Set Your Mind on the Goal 179

Exercise 1: Nine Steps for Setting and
Achieving Life-Changing Goals 199

Exercise 2: Determining What You
Really Want. 204

Exercise 3: Ready, Set Your Goals 208

Chapter 8: Techniques for Resetting
the Clock. 215

Exercise: Key Result Areas. 250

Chapter 9: Your Script for Success 255

Exercise: Emulate Powerful People 307

Chapter 10: The Art of Selling and Closing 319

Chapter 11: Handling Objection
and Rejection 367

Chapter 12: Lead Like You Want to be Lead . . . 391

Chapter 13: The Sum of Everything Within 415

Foreword

> *"The winds of adversity will blown on everyone's boat. It's how we adjust our sails that makes the difference."*

That saying has stayed with me ever since I heard it from the great Jim Rohn. I remember like it was yesterday.

I was stuck in a job thinking of everything I was missing in my life. I wanted so badly to take the giant leap into entrepreneur-ville but I was so worried about failing.

I worried about those same winds of adversity and how they could potentially capsize my boat.

It was also at this moment that I realized if I ever wanted to make something more of myself, I needed to work on my mindset. I could not let those negative beliefs sabotage my dreams. The toxic thoughts needed to leave my mind and be replaced with positive visions of a new, successful me.

Fortunately, I figured this out and through lots of hard work, dedication and a never-say-die mindset success found me.

Fast forward twenty years.

I now speak on stages worldwide sharing my passion for living your dream. I have met thousands of people from all walks of life. Some have realized their dream, some have yet to begin the journey, but all are filled with desire. Out of all of them, one person jumped out at me: Angele Charbonneau.

When I first met Angele, I knew she owned a successful business but I had no idea the journey she had taken to get to that level of success.

To say that Angele has developed a mindset for success is akin to saying the planet Mercury is a little on the warm side.

Angele has come from absolutely nothing and arrived at a lifestyle most people can only imagine for themselves. She was not born with a silver spoon in her mouth. She was not anointed with holy water and given the keys to the financial vault. Angele has worked 20 hour days, while going to school and raising children with her husband.

Angele has mastered the mind to the point where she now laughs in the face of adversity. There is no challenge she will not accept and no person she will turn away when asking for help. When you plug into Angele's wisdom, you will feel like you can climb Mount Everest twice in the same week.

It all begins with our mindset.

When we stand guard at the entrance of our minds, we determine who and what is allowed in.

There is no room for negativity and worry. If they dare to enter the front door, they are immediately shown the exit. When you master your subconscious mind, you reprogram yourself to be the champion you were before you allowed yourself to be guided by negativity and doubt.

It's funny how most kids feel they can conquer anything but somehow by middle age, they just want to make it to Friday. Angele Charbonneau has never lost that childlike passion for success. From running a successful business, to juggling the responsibilities of life and family, she has done it all with style and grace.

The winds of adversity will occasionally blow on your sails, there is no avoiding it. However, with Angele as the captain, there are no rough seas that cannot be conquered.

Sam Crowley
**Speaker, Trainer & Seminar Leader
Founder, Every Day Is Saturday**

Introduction

> *"If you do not change direction, you may end up where you are heading."* – Lao Tzu

It has taken me the majority of my life to figure out what truly makes me happy. There are some people who just seem to know right away what it is they wish to accomplish in life. I've met five-year-olds who were musically gifted and grew up never wavering from their goal of becoming a professional pianist or kids with an exuberant natural curiosity who were sure to become Nobel Prize winning scientists who make a life-changing contribution to the world.

That wasn't me.

After a long journey and a lifelong battle with the ways I was sabotaging myself, today I am secure – in my relationship with my husband and children, in finances, and in my place in the world as an entrepreneur and motivational speaker. I know what my contribution to society is – helping others achieve success – and that gives me a great deal of joy. But it hasn't always been that way, in fact, I've done just about everything possible to disrupt my own happiness. Luckily, I was able to learn from my mistakes. I was able to identify the ways I was fighting the power of intention and reprogram my mind to seek out that which brings me and everyone around me the greatest joy. Now I want to share those secrets with you.

When I left home after high school, I just wanted comfort, enough money to pay the bills and take care of my family, maybe a vacation now and then.

Of course, that's not what I got.

Along the way from then to now I made a lot of sacrifices. I sacrificed my wealth, health and happiness because I thought that was just the way it had to be. I'm here to tell you that it doesn't have to be so hard, if you'll just focus on the right goals and go about achieving them in the right way.

My family is French-Canadian. I grew up in the northern reaches of Canada's eastern coast amongst proud people who toiled endlessly and struggled for what little they had. My parents did their best to raise me and my siblings in that atmosphere, to turn out productive members of society who stay within the law and care for their own, just as they did. It was difficult, at best. We certainly weren't rich but Mom and Dad gave us kids everything they could to provide for our basic needs and then some: financing dancing lessons, sports and hobbies for me and my siblings.

I learned the value of a dollar at a very young age. I learned to work toward my goals, working my first business – a dance studio – at the age of 16. I was taught that the formula for "success" was to go to school, get a job, and pay the bills.

I also formed a lot of beliefs during my childhood, some true but the majority of them false.

It wasn't my parents' fault; they were just raising me the same way they'd been raised. The pattern had been set long before I came along.

I watched Mom and Dad trade time for money, always working hard and never really having enough time or money to spend on the things they wanted or needed. I knew I wanted more than that. They were the hardest working people I ever knew, with incredible work ethics. My siblings and I inherited that trait from them and it would stand us in good stead over the years to come.

I set a goal for myself: to become a chiropractor. In the small town where I grew up, most people saw chiropractors for their health care needs, rather than a physician. I felt this was a noble choice of professions and one that would surely provide the financial stability and respect I so desperately desired.

It took me many long years to reach my goal. I settled down with the man I loved and had my first baby before graduating from university with a Bachelor's degree in Education. Shortly after I made the tough decision to pursue my dream and return to school to become a chiropractor. During my last year of chiropractic school I taught during the day, performed the duties of a chiropractor and mommy in the late afternoons and evening and studied into the wee hours of the morning. Even though I was working hard and hardly sleeping, there were some days we had no more than $20 to our names and had to decide what we could buy for dinner that fit within our meager budget. After four more pregnancies, I then returned to the Michener Institute yet again to receive training in chiropody (referred to as podiatry in the U.S.) which would enhance my chiropractic career.

I took over a clinic in nearby Toronto from a chiropractor who had passed away. I struggled mightily to get the first patient through the door. Eventually, I expanded that first clinic into two, and then into five, most of them located in Toronto. I worked anywhere from seventeen to twenty hours a day, much of it while performing the duties of wife, mother, student, and housekeeper. Luckily, my husband is a great cook and that was one thing I didn't have to add to my plate! I made a lot of money and I lost most of it.

Somewhere along the way between working, going to school, teaching, being a chiropractor and being a mother, I realized that the goals I'd dreamed of throughout my childhood weren't really my ideas of success. That vague thought of success I'd dreamed about as a child was still just that; blurry around the edges.

My husband was (and still is) wonderfully supportive. None of this would have been achievable without him. But after twelve years of me going to school and spending every waking hour working on something for somebody else, our relationship was strained. Date nights and intimate "couch time" were eaten up by my inability to make personal time with my husband a priority. Most nights I got no more than a couple hours sleep while some nights I got none because there just weren't enough hours in the day. Although I never shirked any of my wifely or motherly duties, I had become an automaton, simply trying to get through each day without forgetting one of the hundred tasks I had to accomplish. My husband didn't know who I was anymore. Heck, I didn't know who I was anymore. My life was defined by what I did, not who I was.

The turning point came right after giving birth to my fifth child, Charlize. Most of the people in my life knew that my husband and I were going through a difficult time and had advised us not to have another child. We built a $1.5 million home and although I owned my own business, I was a slave to the clinics because I had to work there ridiculously long hours to pay for it all. I realized that owning my own chiropractic practice was not going to provide financial freedom. I felt like an indentured servant to my business.

After Charlize was born, I had six weeks to spend with my precious newborn and then I had to put my nose back to the grindstone so we could continue to pay our bills.

I woke up one morning and I couldn't look at myself in the mirror, knowing I would have to entrust the care of my baby to someone else so that I could get back to work as quickly as possible and make the mortgage payment on our huge home.

That was it. I couldn't do it any longer. I sat down with my husband and told him we needed to sell the house and if our relationship survived, fine. If not, I could be a single parent. I'd already put myself through so much stress I knew I could raise five kids, bring home the bacon and do the laundry all by myself if I set my mind to it. It wouldn't be the ideal situation, but something had to change. I wanted time and money but I had neither. Maybe without the burden of a huge monthly mortgage payment, I wouldn't feel chained to my business.

I prayed about my decision. At the time, the real estate market in Canada was sluggish, to say the least. We had three realtors take a look at our house and give us a valuation. I insisted that we list the house at $100,000 over the price the agents thought it was worth. If it was meant to be, the house would sell. If not, then we were destined to stay there and come up with a different plan to save my sanity.

In less than twenty-four hours we had an offer on our house for more than the asking price.

That was when I first experienced the incredible, wonderful, positive power of intention.

We took the profit from the sale of that house and invested it in a much smaller, humble little home that ended up being the best place possible for the entire family. My husband stuck around and we worked out our differences. Our relationship actually became better than it ever had been – those struggles and working through them were incredibly beneficial to our growth. I invested some of the home sale profit back into my businesses so that I could create a system that would allow me to work less and spend more time with my family, doing things we all enjoyed. Once again, Friday party time with the kids was something none of us ever missed. Date night returned along with the intimacy I'd once enjoyed with my husband.

Thankfully I got my life turned around in the direction it was meant to go before it was too late.

Now I wake up each morning ready to serve others and make a difference in someone's life – and it feels really good that I am able to do so.

There was a lot to learn from those terribly awful years when nothing seemed to go right. For one thing, I realized that without personal growth, nothing else matters. I couldn't create real wealth until I got my mental house in order and asked for the right things for the right reasons. I also learned that I am resilient. I can fail, and I can bounce back from that failure stronger than before. There is no reason to have a bad attitude when something goes wrong; that just gets in the way of momentum.

The difference between me and others isn't all that big. Many people experience failure and then just give up. I've been very fortunate that I was able to learn from others, grow from my experiences and have a big "why" to keep me going. I have a wonderful family and lots of support from both personal and business contacts. However, I learned from studying the systems of some of the world's most successful people that they perceive failure as something positive. They all have an excellent work ethic, strong desire, lots of commitment and enough motivation to see their goals through to the end. I wanted to be like them and today I am!

Many people – and you might be one of them – just can't seem to get ahead. You may struggle to achieve anything, whether it's a date with an attractive acquaintance or a bigger house or a good income. You probably think you are doing everything right and attribute your problems to circumstances outside your control. Obstacles crop up right and left. Failure to achieve your goals makes your self-esteem suffer, the problems worsen, and the cycle of struggling against the tough forces of nature continues unabated.

It won't get any better until you understand there is only one thing standing in the way of your success and joy: you. When you can't seem to get ahead no matter how hard you try, you must be focusing your energy and effort in the wrong direction, allowing your ego to take over. If your life isn't what you want it to be, your thoughts have not been in alignment with your goals.

In this modern age, we have the misguided notion that success is something we need to hunt down and capture. We believe that if we say the right things, do the right things, take exactly the right steps, success will fly right into our little butterfly net and we can pin it down on a sheet of cardboard and hang it proudly on the wall.

Truthfully, we can't capture success, nor can we buy it, stumble across it, or fall into it. We can only create it, from the inside out. And the only way to create it is by changing our thoughts and habits.

At the beginning of this book I shared what really brings me joy and that is helping others. This time it's your turn. I want to help you decide what it is you really want from life and then teach you how to achieve it. It's not going to be an easy process or a smooth one. You will be rejected. You are bound to experience failure and will certainly feel fear. But by the time you reach the end of this book, you will learn the positive ways to overcome waves and swells on your voyage to success. You will be able to identify a "why" so big that your motivation to attain your goals will never falter. You will define success by your own terms and that will bring you joy.

There is a formula. Did you know that just by changing your mindset, you can begin to effortlessly attract the success you desire? It's true, and reading this book is the first positive decision you can make to start working toward the goal of personal success, however you define it. This book represents the secret code to unlocking the door to success, which can be applied to your professional or personal life, health, relationships – whatever area you desire to change for the better.

The only thing you need is an open mind. The mind is like a parachute – it only works when it's open. Get ready to unlearn self-limiting beliefs and replace them with supportive, positive affirmations. It's not lack of information that stands in the way of your success, but what you *don't know* you don't know! You must be aware in order to change.

And you must be willing to invest the necessary time and effort in yourself to learn the right way to go about achieving your goals. What you expect to see, you see. What you expect to have in your life, you have. What you focus on the most, expands. You need to learn how to transform your thinking processes and develop a truly successful mindset. And with the right mindset, there is no limit to the joy and success you can create in your life.

Everything in life happens for a reason and a purpose. There is a reason you are reading this book at this very minute. Eighty percent of people will start doing the things I've prescribed here but never complete the entire process. Will you take the action necessary to change your life? Are you ready to set a course on an incredible voyage to true fulfillment? Then turn the page…

Chapter One:
Getting Your Mind Onboard With Your Goals

> *"It's the repetition of affirmations that leads to belief. And once that belief becomes a deep conviction, things begin to happen."*
> – Muhammad Ali

Many of us go through life believing that we should want success, that we should have goals. We believe – and we dream. Yet it never gets any farther than that. Our goals remain merely dreams because we can't seem to start our voyage to success. So often we think we are willing to do whatever it takes but when it comes time to take action, we draw back out of fear or temerity or trepidation.

What, then, can we do to make ourselves take that first step? It all starts from within our heads; we need to get our brains onboard with our desires to work toward what we really want out of life.

It comes down to one truth: our minds are in control of our achievements. This can be detrimental, if we harbor negative beliefs, or it can be beneficial, if we learn to overcome self-limiting beliefs and replace them with positive affirmations.

Success is something we can attract if we just set our minds to it. That's an incredible insight that bears repeating: if you change your mindset, you can attract the success you want and deserve.

First, however, you must find the peace within yourself that makes it possible. Inner peace is a function of the subconscious mind; it occurs when all of those extraneous thoughts that often dominate our waking hours are put to rest, and we become centered in our beings. Positive mental change comes about only when we are calm, centered and peaceful, no matter what may be blocking our paths.

Before we can work on establishing mental peace, it's important to understand how our minds work for us, and against us, in terms of goal achievement. Once we realize the role of the conscious and subconscious parts of our brains, we can better control what goes on in there!

The Subconscious Mind

Think of the subconscious part of your mind as the junk drawer in your kitchen cabinets; it's the place where your mind stores everything that it's not consciously thinking about. When you open that drawer, you are sure to find a wide assortment of items based on your past experiences including personal beliefs, memories, skills, situations (good or bad, exciting or dreadful) and even images (particularly things that made a large or negative impact like photos taken at a most inopportune time) – all the things you've experienced in the past that were memorable enough to get stored in your brain's memory bank.

Beliefs can be non-supportive and self-limiting. Although they are not fact or fiction, but merely strong opinions, beliefs color our thoughts and actions with their broad, aggressive brush strokes. They can empower us or they can inhibit forward movement. They can support us or they can drag us backward to a "safe" place filled with nothing to fear, nothing to get anxious about…and nothing to get excited about.

It's been estimated that the typical person's mind goes through fifty thousand thoughts in a single day! Some call these often random thoughts the "little voices" (more about those later) in our heads and they can plant both negative and positive ideas in our subconscious. What we show on the outside might look perfect while on the inside we are just as messy as that junk drawer full of miscellaneous trinkets we haven't used in years. That's where we stow the stuff we don't want others to see.

To best understand how the subconscious mind works, think about it in terms of driving a car. If you've ever taught a teenager to drive, you'll certainly be able to relate to how nervous your child can be as she struggles to remember the right things to do in the proper order. While concentrating on getting the moves down, she's likely to be unable to hold a conversation because that takes her mental focus, her conscious mind, away from the task at hand. However, after lots of practice time on both back roads and busy highways, the movements required for driving become second nature. Weeks or months after that initial test drive, your teen can probably chat with her friends in the back seat, carry on another conversation via Bluetooth, and still drive (much as you may wish she wouldn't!). That automatic aspect of driving is like putting the car on auto pilot and that's also the role of the subconscious mind. The tasks involved in driving, when it becomes accustomed, are transferred to the subconscious level where all those automatically triggered, negative emotions such as fear, embarrassment, and trepidation reside.

The conscious mind, on the other hand, is responsible for logic, calculations, and all the thoughts and actions that occur while you are intentionally concentrating on a particular task. While reading this book, for instance, it's your conscious mind that recognizes the words and absorbs their meanings.

That doesn't mean your subconscious is idle, however. Even while concentrating on the task at hand, your subconscious mind is busily working behind the scenes, accepting or rejecting the information you are receiving based on past experiences and your existing perceptions of the world around you.

Way back when you were an infant, from the first day you entered this vast, new world, your mind began forming perceptions. Each new experience was absorbed like a sponge and sent to a specific part of your subconscious mind for later retrieval. At this stage in your life, you had no preconceived notions or knowledge to stop you from thinking that anything was possible.

This is also when beliefs begin forming. Beliefs about ourselves are all predicated on the things we were told as children. If you learn something that is not true, that bit of information is likely to stay with you for many years, perhaps even forever. The child who is told he is lazy will believe he is lazy and not aspire to achievement; the little girl who is called "fat" believes she really is unattractive and thus harbors a poor self body image because she doesn't know any different. It could be you were labeled as stupid or worthless or mean or rude or whatever negative behaviors you once displayed at a young age.

During early childhood years, there are no preexisting beliefs to contradict those statements so they become accepted, and ingrained, whether they are humbling or harmful, thus becoming a self-fulfilling prophecy.

The subconscious mind stores this information away for later reference and that's why these beliefs become severe handicaps later in life. Negative beliefs limit our abilities and can even have an adverse affect on income ("Money doesn't grow on trees."), education ("To get a good job you must go to school."), or activity level ("You'll never get a job on a Major League baseball team so there's no point practicing your pitch."). You cannot simply discard the hurtful or untrue messages you absorbed during your early life. Sorry, but it's just not that easy. They can be overcome, but it takes effort.

For the longest time I had a problem with money. I would constantly think about it – mainly my lack of it. In order to get past the debilitating little voice in my head that said I would never have money, I had to go back to my subconscious and find those instances when my "money blueprint" had been created. It came directly from generation upon generation of bad conditioning, beliefs that were passed down from my great-grandparents to their children and finally to my parents. They, in turn, having not learned any differently, transmitted those false beliefs about wealth to me and my siblings. For example, my parents often told us that money doesn't grow on trees, or "We can't afford it" when any of us longingly eyed a new toy in the window of the five and dime. We grew up believing that we should never have everything we wanted because there were always other, more important things that claimed top priority in the budget.

When I left home to attend chiropractic school my mother's words would again cement those old beliefs about money in my head. Out of pure love, she told me that when I got rich, I would not want to associate with my family members because I would be a part of the "elite class" and they would not fit in. She meant it with all the love in her heart, wishing the very best for me, but it cut deep. I certainly didn't want to abandon my family if I got rich! I didn't want to think I was better than them; I loved them!

I took these long-held family beliefs literally. Anytime I made more money than I really needed, I gave it away.

It didn't matter how much income I earned. I simply couldn't become wealthy because I felt I didn't deserve to be. As a result, I continuously gave away my money until I consciously changed my subconscious mind. There was really only one reason I wasn't wealthy, and that was because I believed I didn't deserve it.

This is just one example of a single belief that stood in the way of my success. By the time a person is seven or eight years old, he already has a solid foundation with various beliefs in place. For example, he knows whether something is right or wrong, based on conditioning from family, friends, television shows, school teachers, and a host of other environmental influences.

The lesson here is that when things aren't going smoothly in your business or personal life, look within yourself for resolution before placing the blame elsewhere. It may be your own beliefs stopping you from success, whether those beliefs dictate how much money you make, what you eat, what type of spouse you should have, or what you must do on a daily basis to avoid bad luck.

Your subconscious mind may be in control of your destiny and chances are it's got you set on a course of destruction. You could be sabotaging all your efforts to find success either personally or professionally and not even be aware of it. You are limiting yourself based on what you believe to be true, even if it is false or simply misguided.

Just remember that the conclusions we draw about our abilities to succeed or grow are based on what we learned as children, but that doesn't make them valid. Your beliefs will become self-fulfilling prophecies only if you allow them.

Reprogramming the Subconscious Mind

There is good news! Your subconscious mind is the auto pilot feature of your brain, steering your actions away from the path of the unknown. But it can be reprogrammed so that your conscious mind takes over the wheel. You can identify those beliefs that have limited your abilities and then deviate from the current, unsuccessful path you are following in order to get on the right track.

Self-limiting beliefs are stored below your level of conscious awareness. You are only made aware of their existence when they conflict with new thoughts or information. Those old, programmed messages are likely to stand in the way of your best efforts to find success because they don't agree with the new thought that you can achieve anything you set your mind to. They conflict with the new conditions you wish to create, whether that involves wealth, personal relationships, health, or any number of positive things you wish to happen.

Don't be fooled into thinking that something told to you repeatedly throughout childhood is the only thing standing in the way of your success. Our minds are constantly taking in new information and forming new beliefs based on what we are told by others or what we trust is true. It's a never-ending mental process. With each new experience in our lives, we draw new conclusions and store them as data that guides future actions.

You could be very confident about your business acumen, for instance, but end up losing your self-owned company tomorrow. Your subconscious mind, being the clever detective that it is, will search your memory bank for similar instances when some other venture you started didn't turn out so hot. It could go all the way back to the realization of when your childhood lemonade stand ended up costing you more money than it earned. Then you remember that as a teenager, your boss at the fast food restaurant gave you a bad review because you couldn't accurately make change. Eventually, you come to believe that you are just not worthy of having your own business due to your past mistakes. In most cases it couldn't be farther from the truth, but if your subconscious frames it in a way that confirms you are destined to fail, you are likely to have created just one more roadblock on the path to success. This is often referred to as confirmation bias.

Confirmation bias is a way that your crafty mind works to support ingrained principles. If you have a new experience that conflicts with an already established belief, your subconscious mind will either reject it or reframe it so it does go along with your existing viewpoint. That's right – your mind is capable of twisting things to fit into preconceived categories.

Let's say you've been told all your life that you are fat and hideous and that has become a deep-seated component of your psyche. When a good-looking person comes along and expresses an interest in getting to know you better, your subconscious mind will find reasons to disbelieve the truth or innocence of the situation. You are likely to think that it was set up as some sort of cruel joke or perhaps it is just a moment of insanity on the other person's part. There is no way you can believe that someone could possibly find you attractive. That simply doesn't fit into your belief system. You might reject the interested party before he or she can reject you. Chances are you will somehow damage what could have been a potentially great relationship.

The power of your subconscious mind works to make whatever happens in your life support what you believe. When you cannot attain your goals, you start to believe that you simply aren't capable of success. If you come to expect failure of yourself you will end up doing just that – failing – over and over again.

Turning Your Beliefs Around

The good news? There is life after self-limiting beliefs and you can harness the power of the subconscious mind for your own benefit.

Once you reprogram your self-limiting subconscious beliefs, you can literally change your life. Believe you can have money and that it will come to you easily. Believe that you are good-looking and worthy of attracting the attention of someone else.

When you turn your beliefs around, you will naturally get what it is you desire. Truly, you can achieve just about anything when you take the time to reprogram your subconscious mind.

First, you must identify non-supportive beliefs in order to change them. Letting go of handicaps often requires working through painful memories, but it's a necessary part of getting past them and it can be quite freeing. Don't expect to automatically change your subconscious mind and thus your underlying beliefs about your own worth as a human being. However, you can consider this the beginning of the process of conscious and positive change.

The following exercise will get you thinking about your personal negative belief system and determining ways you can overcome this impediment.

EXERCISE: Reprogramming Self-Limiting Beliefs

Your self-image is formed from a set of inner beliefs about yourselves. These beliefs are based upon past experiences and what we determined they meant at the time they occurred.

I want you to explore the beliefs that form your current self-image because they will determine your thoughts, feelings, behaviors – and ultimately your level of success in all things.

Your self-limiting beliefs may include some of the following:

- "I don't have what it takes to be successful."
- "I'm just not a people person."
- "No matter what I do, I can't seem to get ahead."
- "I'm unattractive and no one would want to be with me."
- "I stink at math."
- "I'm terrified of public speaking."
- "I could never be an airplane pilot because I'm afraid of heights."
- "I can't be a doctor because I flunked science in middle school."

It's very easy to buy into these "excuses" (yes, that's what they are!) because they remove the responsibility from our shoulders. Convincing ourselves that we're just "not good" at something means we no longer have to try hard or take risks. It's out of our hands. Consequently, we hold ourselves back from the lives we really wish we were living. We feel stuck in a vicious cycle of frustration fueled by the desire for something more or better, but not believing we are able to, or deserve to, attain it. Now is the time to overcome that frustration.

Exercise: Make sure you have at least fifteen minutes to yourself. Get into a comfortable position. Read over the following paragraphs once, then close your eyes and perform the actions as described.

1. Think back to a time in your life when you felt powerless, small, weak, rejected, unloved, inferior, worthless, like you had no meaning.

Perhaps it was in grade school when someone laughed at you.

Maybe you weren't the cool kid and ate lunch alone every day.

Perhaps your parents, siblings, relatives or friends said something that made you doubt your abilities or skills or stamina or motivation.

Maybe you grew up seeing stuff no child should: your parents violently quarreling, a lack of respect or love between family members, substance abuse, dangerous living conditions, etc.

Maybe you were unjust to someone or someone was unjust to you and you never got a chance to resolve the issue.

Maybe you are disappointed by wrong choices you made because others didn't believe in you.

Take a moment and go back to a time where someone or something affected you in a profound way.

2. Describe the scene. Return to that situation and think about what you were wearing, the scenery around you, how the other people involved were situated and how they looked. Can you see yourself? Can you see your face? What emotions are you experiencing? How do you feel?

You were afraid; unable to deal with the situation back then because it was beyond your control but not today.

3. Right here and right now you can decide to take a different path, to reset the course of your life. Perhaps it is the path of forgiveness, the path of standing up for what is right, or the path of finding a good job no matter the circumstances.

Choose to stop being the victim, right here, right now. Replace that self-limiting belief with a new, positive one. You can make friends. You are attractive. You do know how to manage people. You are smart, savvy, good and kind.

Find the inner peace in the center of your mind and relax into the moment.

Close your eyes and recall the experience brought to mind.

Then open your eyes and write down the self-limiting belief you just envisioned. Remember what you did to overcome the circumstances you relived.

Write down this new outcome so you can refer back to how it felt to overcome a self-limiting belief.

When you doubt that you can do anything, remember this inner-centered peace you just lived and go back to it!

Chapter Two:
Steer Your Mind Toward Success

> *"Choosing to be positive and having a grateful attitude is going to determine how you're going to live your life."* – Joel Osteen

You can set the GPS system in your car to take the most direct route or one that avoids freeways. Perhaps you prefer the scenic route that will take you past popular tourist attractions.

The same way that you point your car to the route you wish to take from Point A to Point B is also much the same way you can reprogram your mind to find success.

We know that our belief system is a product of our personal experiences and that it resides in the subconscious mind. Those negative beliefs are detrimental; they function as roadblocks on the path to success, whether that success is defined as a personal or professional triumph.

Replacing negative, self-limiting beliefs with positive, self-empowering ones is actually fairly simple. All it requires is the determination to keep at it. Practice makes perfect, as the old saying goes, and this is indeed true when it comes to making positive affirmations part of your everyday life. The following ways of overcoming negative beliefs are simple methods of replacing the wicked with the worthy and ones that you can easily include in your daily routine.

Replace Negative Thoughts

We all have thoughts. We all have those nagging little voices inside our heads telling us all the things we can't do. But if you are ever going to succeed at anything, you must stop being a victim of your self. Stop letting negativity control your life.

I'll bet you know at least one Debbie Downer. She could be a family member, a co-worker, an employee or even a friend. She's the person who sees the negative in everything, a real "glass half empty" kind of gal. Why does she see the dark side of everything? It's because she chooses to be dominated by negativity.

On what we allow our thoughts to dwell, is both a choice and a habit. You can learn to turn your mind to the positive in every situation just as easily as you can condition yourself to always see the negative. What choice would you wish to make?

The first step in changing a habit is becoming aware of it. As you go through your day, make a conscious effort to identify negative thoughts as they occur then replace them with opposite, constructive thoughts.

For example, if you find yourself thinking that you'll never be successful because you just can't seem to break out of your limiting behaviors, consciously affirm that you have just as much potential to be successful as anyone else. Tell yourself, "I am successful." That's not, "I could be successful" or "I might find success eventually." Say this statement in the present tense in order to make it a part of your present circumstances.

Affirmations

Affirmations are positive declarations that confirm the attainment of a goal. They are more than just motivational buzzwords; with repetition and practice they can actually change your life.

Repeating positive affirmations works incredibly well in regard to changing your subconscious mind, whether it likes it or not!

However, most people suffer from a lack of commitment. If you've tried this method before and found it ineffective, the problem could be with your level of stick-to-itiveness; it takes months, not just days, to see real change happen. If you won't commit to daily affirmations for more than a week or so I would advise you not to start in the first place and save yourself the frustration.

There is no such thing as a negative affirmation; affirmations are always positive and always in the present tense. So, instead of saying "I will be confident and successful one day" it is much more affirming – and much more likely to provoke a timely change in behavior – to say, "I am confident and successful." Focusing on a future condition has no effect on the subconscious mind, which is only aware of present circumstances.

It is also important to word affirmations in a positive manner and avoid statements such as "I am not a failure." To your subconscious mind, you are actually saying, "I am a failure." Reword that affirmation as, "I am a success!"

While you are verbalizing your positive affirmation, call up the corresponding feeling. Telling yourself, "I am wealthy" while turning out your pockets and finding only a handful of change sends conflicting messages to your subconscious. Strive to really feel the message as well as say it and your mind will be more apt to actually believe it.

Affirmations are meant to be repeated, over and over again. For some people it's not enough to say them once a day; it can be much more effective if they are repeated throughout. There's no need to say them out loud; simply saying them to yourself is quite effective, and this can be done anytime, anywhere. Positive affirmations can very simply become a part of your daily routine, much as you would brush your teeth or comb your hair.

Believe in Yourself

You may have heard the phrase, "you are who you think you are." Working on transforming the quality of your thoughts can help you develop a strong belief in yourself and your abilities.

Start by making a list of all the positive characteristics, traits, qualities, skills and talents you possess. Write down everything positive you can think of; if you are having a difficult time with this, ask someone who loves you to help compile the list. Even if you don't believe your talents are all that amazing, the things you can do well are still a positive aspect of your personality.

Spend some time each day reviewing the list and affirming your ability to accomplish whatever it is you set out to do.

Over time you will feel more positive about yourself and more confident about your abilities just because you've developed the habit of believing so.

Visualization

The best way to form a positive habit is to utilize all your senses, but there's one sense that makes a particularly big difference. The fact is that most of us are visual learners. Using the power of visualization is an extremely effective method of changing your subconscious mind. The more times you repeat your positive visions, the clearer the picture of your success becomes and the faster you will see results.

Although we are discussing positive affirmations, I want to make you aware of a negative way we sabotage the reprogramming of self-limiting beliefs, and that's by watching television. If you truly want to turn things in your life around, you must quit watching TV shows and particularly news programs, which are filled with negativity, hatred, despair, war, violence, crime, pain and poverty. While watching the tube, you absorb all the negative statistics and you end up becoming one yourself.

You may not be aware of it but your subconscious mind is feeding on everything it sees and hears from the moment you are born to the moment you die. The best thing you can do in regard to changing your subconscious mind is to feed it only positive energy. Think only affirmative thoughts about anything, as long as it is not harmful or depressing.

Learn to Love Yourself

You may wonder what self-love has to do with success. More than you can imagine! Self-love and self-worth go hand in hand. If you don't believe you are worthy of success, you will keep pushing it away or find ways to interfere with your goals and thus prevent yourself from attaining them.

The key to overcoming negative feelings about yourself is to engage in positive self-talk on a consistent basis. That means telling yourself something good each and every day. Rather than tearing yourself down over something you did badly or wrong, choose to fill your inner dialogue with empowering affirmations. Build yourself up with phrases like, "You were really kind to Sue in Accounting today when you helped her file all those old invoices." Even if you lost a big account during a sales presentation, focusing on something you did right makes you much more apt to repeat that positive behavior in the future because you are retraining your subconscious mind to provide a reward for it.

There is no reason you can't treat yourself with the same love and respect you show to others. Think of how you would speak to a beloved parent or child. Would you sound cruel and unforgiving?

Would you remind them of their weaknesses or rub their faces in their failures?

It doesn't matter how others treat you or what they say to you. All that really matters is how you treat yourself – and you deserve at least as much respect as anyone else. Ironically, the better you treat yourself, the more you will find that others see you in a consistently positive light and ultimately treat you better, too. It's all about what you believe you deserve.

Treating yourself with love and kindness also means you must shift your focus from what you don't want (negative) to what you do want (positive). If your biggest fear is failure, your subconscious mind will motivate you to avoid that possibility at all costs. That may show itself as procrastination and an avoidance of risk taking. If, instead, you focus your thoughts on being successful at whatever you do, you'll find that your fear of failure diminishes.

It's all about the power of attraction: the more you focus on what you want, the less you will attract what you don't want.

Get to Know the Real You

It's difficult, if not impossible, to turn your negative beliefs into positive thoughts of success if you don't really know how you define success. It's a personal concept different for each and every one of us. Only by getting in touch with our true passions, hopes, dreams, and aspirations can we identify those things that personally define success. And it's definitely not about what our parents or spouses believe to be valuable or worthwhile. It's all about you.

Those preconceived notions of what you can and cannot do, which lie deep in your subconscious mind, could be sidetracking your attainment of real joy and achievement. Maybe someone in your past called you a terrible writer and squashed your dream of becoming an author. Just because you received criticism of one written work long ago doesn't mean you can't write a book today. Just because you tried it once and it didn't work isn't a good enough excuse to shelf your passion.

The truth is you can become good or even great at anything if you want it badly enough and you are willing to put the time and effort into getting there.

Some people have a difficult time identifying their dreams and passions. If that's you, vow to spend more time with yourself, and only yourself.

Many people fear this. They don't enjoy spending time alone because they are fearful of uncovering true emotions. If you've never taken yourself out to dinner or a movie, learn how to do it at least once, preferably more. The more time you spend getting in touch with yourself, the more connected you become to your deepest emotions and feelings. You begin to tap into your inner dialogue, and a more intimate understanding of who you truly are will surface.

Forgive Yourself

Many of us find it easy to forgive others but impossible to provide that same forgiveness to ourselves. But you cannot move forward, toward a better life filled with positive affirmations, until you let go of the junk in your subconscious that's holding you back.

You may feel guilty about allowing fear to keep you from achieving goals, for treating someone badly in the past, for not believing in yourself, for allowing other people to define who you are.

Now is the time to let all that go. Affirm that you did the best you knew how to do at the time, those guilty feelings arose, and it's now time to move on. Now you know better and you won't make those same mistakes again.

Begin a daily habit of encouraging yourself. Remember to be kind to yourself and affirm your ability to accomplish anything you want. Eventually, you will actually begin to believe it and your life will start to change.

While going through the process of forgiving yourself, don't forget to absolve others for any wrongdoings they have done to you in the past. Others are likely to have harmed you, belittled you, or held you back from achieving your dreams. You can't change them, but you can forgive them for acting in a way that caused you pain. Although these experiences may have affected you in profound ways, they do not have the ability to influence you now or control your life's path – unless you choose to allow them that power.

Let go of your anger, hurt, disappointment and bitterness. These negative emotions do nothing for you and actually work against you. They punish you by acting as a heavy burden adding unnecessary weight to your life's journey. When you release negative emotions, you free yourself to experience the joy and create the success you truly deserve.

Remember that the only way to change your outer world is to first change your inner world.

How to Tell if Your Mind Has Changed

Since you can't actually see your subconscious mind, you may have a hard time determining if it's really changing due to your efforts. You can't peek inside and see if there's still a bunch of garbage banging around in the drawer! What you can do, however, is to develop better self-awareness. Learn to recognize the signs of progress, which may include:

- You begin feeling stronger, more confident and happier.
- You find yourself more willing to take risks and face new challenges.
- Your dreams and goals don't seem overwhelming anymore, just exciting.
- You feel a deeper sense of inner peace, as if inner conflicts have dissolved.
- You attract more opportunities to expand and grow in every area of your life.

One thing you can't expect is instant change. Reprogramming your subconscious takes time, consistency and persistence. Just as it took you weeks or even months to create a new habit, it will take the same level of dedication to go through all your subconscious junk and toss out the negative, self-limiting beliefs for good.

Choose your reprogramming methods and install positive messages in your subconscious day after day, week after week. When the transformation becomes apparent, you will be motivated to keep moving forward. Until that happens, stay true to the course and keep advancing forward one step at a time to make positive, powerful changes that last a lifetime.

Reprogramming Tips and Techniques

Finally, here are a few simple tips and techniques you can perform on a daily basis to keep your subconscious reprogramming goals on track.

Be the Guardian of Everything That Enters Your Mind

The old motto, "garbage in, garbage out" is so true, particularly when it comes to your subconscious. Everything you see and hear and feel fuels your subconscious mind. It's up to you to manage what goes in there and keep it clean and pure, which is more effective than trying to purge negative information once it is firmly rooted in your subconscious.

Eliminate negative input as much as you can by limiting the amount of news you read, violent movies you watch, and graphic images you see. Make a conscious effort to seek out positive information and allow it to flow through your mind. Your subconscious will naturally become more positive when it is fueled by affirmative thoughts.

Set Aside Time Just for You

Are you any less important than the paperwork in the office or the dirty laundry in the hamper? Everyone needs regular periods of time in which to reflect privately. Set aside an hour each day just for you to pray, meditate, practice yoga or read something positive, without interruption. Your subconscious mind needs to know how important you are. Nothing indicates this better than making time to treat yourself to positive input.

I encounter a lot of people who balk at this suggestion. They believe they simply cannot find a free hour each day for themselves. If I can accomplish this while performing the duties of a wife, mother, business owner, student, and speaker, then so can you. Whether you have to wake up earlier or go to bed later than usual, experiencing a calming hour just for you each day is vitally important to clearing your thoughts and becoming open to the exciting new possibilities your subconscious mind can offer.

Speak Kindly to Yourself

When you look in the mirror do you like what you see? Do you compliment yourself on your most outstanding attributes?

Stop all negative, self-doubting, self-limiting talk immediately. Remind yourself of all your wonderful qualities or abilities, such as your great eyes, your winning smile, your uncanny knack for getting people to open up – whatever sets you apart from others in a positive way.

Success really does come from within. It's up to you to change your mindset and overcome disabling beliefs that hold you back from success. Take the time to perform the following exercises now, while the concept of positive affirmation is still fresh in your mind, and watch the changes start to happen.

Exercise 1: Replace the Negative with a Positive

Let's start with a simple exercise that you can do once but refer to time and time again.

Simply make a list of your most common negative thoughts and then counter each one with a positive.

Example:

<u>Negative</u>	<u>Positive</u>
I'll never have enough money to buy a house.	I'll set aside $X each week until I've saved up enough for a down payment on a house.

Not sure what to write in each column? Start journaling. Record your thoughts, feelings, struggles, fears and dreams each and every day. Ask yourself questions and answer them. This will remind you of the things you worry about and allow you to work through solutions while you are calm and centered.

In addition to writing down negative and positive emotions, write down five things you are grateful for each day. These written, positive affirmations can be reviewed as often as necessary to quickly change your mood from pessimistic to optimistic in mere seconds.

Exercise 2: Creative Visualization

Another wonderful tool for forming new beliefs is using your imagination to change your self-image. Visualization is an easy yet effective tool to replace your old, limiting self-image with an empowering, new one. You simply close your eyes and create a mental image of yourself as you wish to be.

Your subconscious mind responds well to pictures. Visualization is a great way to program your mind with positive, empowering images.

Here are some things you may want to visualize:

- An abundance of money
- Fulfilling relationships
- Passionate work
- A slender, fit body
- A beautiful home
- An expensive car
- Exotic vacations

Anything else you wish to draw into your life

See yourself as confident, inspired, courageous, and successful. See yourself changing the situation that left you powerless, rejected, disbelieving, bereft of hope, etc.

As you do this exercise consistently, you end up redrawing the negative pictures from your past experiences, fears, worries, and doubts stored in your subconscious junk drawer. Your subconscious mind will absorb the messages as if they are real! This is the true beauty of visualization – the power to bypass limiting messages and focus on pleasing images, all of which are being integrated with your subconscious to be played back at a later time.

To boost the power of visualization even further, be sure to emit strong, positive emotions while you picture these wonderful things in your mind. Allow feelings of love, joy, gratitude, and peace to flow through you as if you were truly having these experiences. Before long, you'll find that you won't have to manufacture these feelings; you will feel this way nearly all the time – naturally!

Try spending 10-15 minutes a day visualizing positive scenes that feature you and your new life experiences. Alternately, you can work on creative visualization in smaller chunks: three times a day for just three minutes at a time.

This is doable and it quickly creates a positive daily habit.

Chapter Three:
Thinking Past Your Comfort Zone

> *"A dream is your creative vision for your life in the future. You must break out of your current comfort zone and become comfortable with the unfamiliar and the unknown."* – Denis Waitley

Have you read a book and imagined how much better it would be using your own ending? Have you ever people watched at the mall and imagined what you would do if you were that person walking by wearing a leather jacket and a sultry smile? Then you, my friend, are ready to learn how to think past your comfort zone and start seeing new results.

I remember graduating from the Canadian Memorial Chiropractic College, holding my freshly inked degree in one hand, and basking in the joy of making it through the complete course load to become certified as a chiropractor. It was a feeling of pure euphoria. Finally, all those years of sacrificing sleep and sanity culminated in the moment when I could open my own clinic, become my own boss, and make my own rules.

I bought the practice of a deceased chiropractor in Toronto who, by the end of his career and life, had lost all his patients. I paid one dollar for the business, which didn't include the office space it was located in. Although there were a lot of things I could have used, I didn't apply for a loan because I knew I wouldn't even qualify for $10,000 due to the amount of student debt I'd amassed.

I'll never forget holding the key to the front door, my hand shaking with excitement as I inserted it into the lock and turned the knob. Here it was – my very own practice! Now I'd truly made it. No more having to worry about money, no more long nights with an hour of sleep at best. I had arrived.

Euphoria quickly turned into alarm.

I used what little money I had to make the place look awesome via a fresh coat of paint, and a thorough cleaning. I set up my office, placing plants on the windowsill and filling shelves with medical books. It was comfortable in that space and exactly how I had pictured my first clinic when I was just a young girl dreaming of becoming a chiropractor. I sat in the same chair the old chiropractor had, the leather cracked and worn from years of use but as comfortable as an old friend.

Then I waited. And waited. No one came through the door.

After a few weeks went by, I began to panic. The rent on the building was due and I had yet to make a dime. I didn't have any patients…now what was I going to do? That place of comfort I'd found quickly turned into the zone of terror. Either I could take a deep breath and push past my comfort zone into new territory to quickly find some paying patients, or I could wallow there in that office, waiting to be kicked out for nonpayment. I chose option number one.

No matter what your religious beliefs, I can confidently state that there are no such things as accidents. Whether you are Christian or Muslim, Protestant or Buddhist, we all agree there is a higher power in control of the universe and most of us believe He is in control of our fate.

I know you are reading this book for a reason and I would have to guess it's because you've made a commitment to yourself to grow personally and/or professionally, to learn and live with a greater purpose to serve and help others. If that's true, then there is no time like the present to get started.

We've already discussed the role of the subconscious mind as the keeper of beliefs based on past experience. But another part of our minds functions in the primary role of keeping us safe and protected. It's programmed to keep us squarely and firmly in the comfort zone (CZ).

In fact, I like to refer to the CZ as our own self-created prison, a place where we are always at ease with our personal and professional lives, doing what we know how to do best. It's like a well-lighted rest stop on the side of a busy highway, a place where we can relax without feelings of risk or anxiety.

However, the CZ is also the place that prevents us from getting where we really want to go: the Money Zone, the Health Zone and the Wealth Zone. Inside the prison of our CZ there is no room for personal or professional growth. It's a stagnant place where nothing ever changes and people don't grow (much like that old practice I bought!).

Every single one of us has a personal CZ, along with built-in mechanisms that regulate the levels of anxiety, fear and discomfort we experience. Thinking outside of the box and then moving just one inch out of the comfort zone's existing boundaries causes a feeling of anxiety. The minute that anxious feeling starts to kick in, we back peddle and high tail it back to the place we know best; it's our natural tendency as human beings. Remember, our minds are conditioned to keep us in the nice, safe place where new situations can't threaten us.

The CZ clearly and instantly shows us how much fear and anxiety we can, or can't tolerate. It causes sweaty palms, stomachaches, and a general feeling of dread. It's why we often say to ourselves, "Ugh. I've gotta do this but I really don't want to."

To prevent these feelings, your mind keeps you well within the boundaries of your self-made prison. It comes up with all sorts of excuses why you can't accomplish what it is you really don't want to do.

So why can't you stay in your CZ and feel nice and safe? Well, you could...but if you don't push past the boundaries of your CZ, you will never grow personally or professionally.

I'm going to tell you right now that it is not easy to get out of your CZ. You can be cocky, brash, and assertive but still long for the peaceful feelings you experience within your CZ. That's just the way we are made. Luckily, it doesn't have to control our lives or dictate our chances of success. It just requires a bit of effort and stamina to push past the boundaries.

That's exactly what I had to do in order to grow my chiropractic practice. I decided that what I needed to do was introduce myself to the community as the new chiropractor, to hand out business cards and kiss babies.

I had a chance to do just that shortly after hanging out my shingle, I was invited by a friend of mine to join a local golf tournament. My first thought was that it would be an excellent opportunity to network with some really influential people; to enjoy some one-on-one time with movers and shakers in my community who could spread the word about my business and send patients my way. Even better, those same movers and shakers would probably need an adjustment after a day out on the golf course and guess who I could recommend?

My second thought was, "Oh my God! I don't know the first thing about golf!"

You see, I'm not an athletic type of person. Never have been. And last I checked, golf was still considered a sport.

My friend called a couple days prior to the event to make sure I was still going. I wanted to say yes but my CZ did the talking. "No, I can't. Um...I'll find someone to replace me."

The moment I entertained actually playing golf, heck, the moment I heard the word "golf", my stomach balled up into knots of anxiety. Whacking away at a tiny white ball on a field of green would be going way beyond my CZ.

I had to break out of my CZ. After all, rent was due.

I took a deep breath and reminded myself that how you do anything is how you do everything. If I failed to take part in the golf tournament, it would mean my practice might never be successful due to fear. What was I thinking, starting my own practice? But...was I really going to give up now? After all those years of sacrifice and hard work, was I going to let it all go over one lousy golf tournament?

Letting my CZ take control of this situation would set a dangerous precedent. If I couldn't get out of my CZ now, I just knew I would never be able to grow my business to the next level. I might as well as tear down my shingle right away rather than prolong the torture.

I forced myself to enter that golf tournament.

Mental alarm bells started sounding the moment I stepped out of my car, signaling that I'd gone far past my CZ. I ignored them and resolutely walked up to the pro shop to rent the necessary equipment – I didn't own a single golf club! I was wearing running shoes and the clothes I use to go jogging each morning, my hair pulled back in a ponytail. I didn't own the proper clothes like the other ladies at the club did. They wore fashionable golf shorts and had their hair styled to look artlessly mussed. They had the right looks, and they knew their way around the course.

Did I learn to play golf by the end of the tournament? Not really. I took a lot of chunks out of the grass and found out they are called divots.

I was undoubtedly the worst player on the course that day.

But you know what? I also met a lot of great people. I forged some valuable new relationships and all in all, had a really good time. By pushing through the boundaries of my CZ, I was rewarded with a network of new friends who helped send patients through my front door. That was the start of some lasting, valuable relationships that continue to this day.

If I can get out of my comfort zone and play golf, you, too, can do whatever it takes to make your business successful! And if you don't push yourself to break those boundaries, you will forever remain mediocre.

Nothing good comes easily. In fact, only 10 percent of people are willing to push their boundaries and achieve their goals and dreams, to become an incredible person who makes a real difference. Inside your CZ it's a big, lonely sphere;

outside of its confines is where all the fun and exciting and good opportunities in your personal and professional life lie in wait for you!

Remember the quote by Denis Waitley used at the beginning of this chapter? "A dream is your creative vision for your life in the future." What do you want next week, next month, next year? You must break out of your current CZ and become more relaxed at the idea of encountering the unfamiliar and the unknown. Only then can you find out what great things await you on the other side.

You may be asking yourself, "What if I can't do this? What if I fail?" Fear of failure is the mental material that comprises the chains of our self-created prisons. Fear has a way of making itself much bigger in our minds than it is in reality. We work ourselves into a sweat, terrified of the "what ifs" when, in fact, the worst outcome you can imagine would probably be no big deal. As with most other things in life, you would simply pick yourself up and continue on your way with nary a scratch.

Another fear that holds us back is the fear of what other people will think. If you are worried about looking good, you will fail. If you refuse to do anything you can't do well or that doesn't make you look good, you will fail. If you never even try you will never, ever reach your goals of success. Don't do this to yourself! There are seven billion people in the world; not all will like who you are or what you do. That's okay. We're all different – and that's a good thing. If I had been afraid to attend that golf tournament because I didn't have the right clothes, hairstyle, or Botoxed lips, I might never have met the huge network of people I did.

Think about it this way: we've all failed at something. And we are going to fail again, I promise! It bears repeating: nothing good comes easily. You almost have to fail in order to achieve success.

Let's consider another statistic: 90 percent of all new businesses will close their doors within the first few years. Is it merely a coincidence that this number matches the amount of people who will never step outside their comfort zones to achieve something worthwhile? I don't think so. Only 10 percent of businesses make it because only 10 percent of us ever become successful entrepreneurs who are willing to go above and beyond and do whatever it takes to make it big. Are you one of them?

It's difficult to push through the walls of your CZ but take heart; each time you manage to get out of your self-imposed CZ prison, it becomes easier and easier.

Use the following exercises to get out of your CZ once and for all, to break the chains and burst through on the other side of success!

Exercise 1: Working Past Anxiety

Before you make any drastic life changes, try to make a simple change in your routine, such as:

- Shopping at a different grocery store.
- Sleeping on the other side of the bed.
- Taking a different route driving home.
- Ordering a new dish at your favorite restaurant .
- Changing your morning routine, such as washing your hair before brushing your teeth.

Even these small changes will feel uncomfortable. You'll get that yucky, queasy feeling in your stomach.

Get in a comfortable, safe place and take a moment to write down the specifics of how you feel. Tell yourself, "I've got to do this".

Allow your anxiety level to increase. Feel your heart rate and breathing get faster, producing adrenaline. Adrenaline is your body's natural drug that, in moderation, makes you sharper, quicker, and more creative. It creates a feeling of excitement and exhilaration that comes from doing something new.

This process can be a bit stressful at first. Let it happen in a safe place first so you can recognize the fear and deal with it when it happens elsewhere, such as your office, a networking event or a conference.

Each time you push the boundaries of your CZ you overcome at least one fear. That fact alone should provide the motivation you need to keep working on breaking through your CZ.

Exercise 2: Exploring Your CZ Boundaries

Set aside some time to do this exercise. Go to a place where you will feel comfortable and can work on this undisturbed for at least 15 minutes, such as behind a closed office door or at home when no one else is there. Read through the exercise, then close your eyes and go through the steps.

Think of something that would totally put you outside your comfort zone if you were asked to do it today. Perhaps it's making an oral presentation in front of dozens or hundreds of people (a very common fear). Maybe it would be dancing or having a conversation with a complete stranger you meet at a business event. It could be cold calling a list of prospective clients or asking your current customers for a really big sale. Whatever makes you most nervous and uncomfortable, concentrate on that one action.

1. Focus on how you are feeling right here, right now. When you think of this action, does your stomach twist into knots, does your heart race, do you feel uneasy, do your palms get sweaty?
2. Picture yourself doing the very action that makes you so uncomfortable, the action that is completely and totally out of your CZ. You may experience tremendous fear but it's okay in this safe time and place.
3. Be aware of all the feelings you are experiencing right here, right now. These are the very feelings that are stopping you from doing what you need to and should be doing. This is showing up in your life in more ways than one.

4. Now, I want you to tell your fear, "Thanks for trying to protect me, but I'm going to do it anyway." Say this to yourself out loud. Then see yourself just do it, again and again.

5. Open your eyes.

The first few times you step out of your comfort zone, you will undoubtedly be distressed. Expect that and accept it. Fear won't vanish overnight. But it will go away after your mind understands that the fear is groundless.

Those who are willing to push their boundaries will do it! It's easier here in your safe place than out there by yourself, so practice now and get used to the feelings in order to deal with them efficiently later.

The point is to stop letting fear make your decisions, and start making conscious decisions on your own terms. It will take some time to get used to this new way of thinking, but before long you'll automatically begin questioning your fear and stop letting it control your life.

Once you know what your fears are, and you understand and accept the consequences, and immediately do the thing you fear most. Yes, that's right, I'm encouraging you to break the chains of your CZ penitentiary right now, today, tomorrow, next week, over and over again! Refuse to let fear control your actions.

If you can do this exercise, you can do anything. Don't worry about what others think about you! It's all about letting it go once and for all!

You must be willing and daring to push the limits of your CZ in order to grow. Each time you do that, you grow exponentially. Your greatest intelligence is not your brain. The highest intelligence in the world is your ability to do what it is you fear most.

Chapter Four:
Get the Car Out of the Garage

> *"I've missed more than nine thousand shots in my career. I've lost almost three hundred games. Twenty six times, I've been trusted to take the game winning shot and missed. I've failed over and over and over again in my life. And that is why I succeed."* – Michael Jordan

What does it take to be successful – to make it all the way from the here and now to future success? Have you ever asked yourself that question? Most of us have pondered the answer but it's not an easy one, nor it can it be summed up in a single word.

The first thing to keep in mind is that you will never go anywhere if you don't first get the car out of the garage!

If you truly want to know the traits, actions and characteristics of successful people, then you must closely examine what it is that most successful people do, how they think, why they remain motivated. Luckily you don't have to do that for yourself; I've got the path to success all plotted out for you. These are the traits you need to start your voyage to success and ultimately arrive at your goals.

1. *Commitment*

Commitment is the founding drive of the entrepreneur, the one trait that fuels everyone's personal success journey. It's not just about telling yourself you can make your dream a reality, but to see it all the way through, past the sleepless nights, and the dwindling bank account. Pushing through your own self-doubt to actually see yourself cross the finish line. To have the satisfaction of looking back and saying, "I did it!" That is true commitment at its finest.

Successful people stay on the path, even if they occasionally take a detour or two, and continually commit. If you want to achieve your goals, you can't let obstacles be insurmountable walls.

Defining a big "why" for what you want to accomplish is vital to maintaining commitment. If I told you that you needed $1 million to pay for a surgery that would save your child's life there's no doubt you would raise the money. After all, your child's life is at stake! The reason behind achieving your goal needs to be so monumental that you will commit to doing whatever it takes. Once you have made the decision to set up your own business, you must follow through with consistency.

Did you ever wish to learn to play a musical instrument, a sport or to speak a foreign language? How long did you stick to your plan? How much time did you spend learning and what did you accomplish? Chances are you started a lot of projects and halfway through the course you quit because things got tough and you lacked the commitment necessary to finish.

The truth is that most people quit as soon as things get difficult. Making a long-term commitment to anything – a spouse, a job, financial security – is not easy. This applies to personal relationships too. Take a look at the divorce rate in North America and you'll understand what I mean.

I struggled with commitment until I finally defined my own big why: being a role model for my children. I couldn't bear the thought of them growing up with the same self-limiting beliefs I had. I didn't want them to struggle to make money and then give it all away like I did. If I was going to change the future of my children, I first had to change myself.

So, before you take on the task of establishing your business, determine whether you are able to make a long-term commitment. Find your big why and use it to motivate your actions for as long as it takes.

2. Determination

The difference between a successful entrepreneur and one who quits is attitude. Where others see failure, the successful entrepreneur sees an opportunity to learn. Mistakes are regarded as a chance for character development, while obstacles are simply minor speed bumps caused by improper timing.

Enterprising businesspeople continue on their quest with great persistence, always looking forward to the moment when their time will come, when they will finally reach their destination:

success. Most of all, they never give up and never quit striving for success. They are persistent, even when the path becomes littered with huge boulders. They find the stamina to shove them aside because nothing can stand in the way of their success.

If the journey to success was easy, everyone would be basking in their wealth. There will always be challenges to face but you must face them with a willingness to learn and a desire to grow.

3. Risk Taking

Do you really want to find success? Then you must do that which causes you the most fear. Entrepreneurs don't view risk as hazardous, they view it as challenging or opportunistic. They know there are no risk-free journeys to success.

Most people believe there are only two choices when they strike out toward a goal of success: to take risks or to not take risks. When they reach a fork in the road, they see one direction as representing safety and the other as danger. It's black and white.

This is not how entrepreneurs weigh the risks of the journey to success. They know that risk is unavoidable, but also realize they have a choice as to which risk they wish to take – one that leads to the loss of replaceable assets or one that leads to the loss of everything important in life. True entrepreneurs choose the former because they perceive that a life is lost if it is lived without significance, meaning, or the attainment of goals.

Entrepreneurs are fearful, but only of a so-called risk-free life that ends in the anguished regret of what might have been, of what could have been, of what should have been. Compared to this life failure, an entrepreneur perceives risk to actually be quite minimal. For the successful entrepreneur, life is not just about surviving, for everyone ultimately fails at that, but to live with purpose. Their mantra is, "If I don't take a chance I will never know what I could have become."

4. Hard Working

Have you ever met a lazy, successful person? I'm not referring to someone who inherited wealth; that's a different story. Even if you are lucky enough to have a successful business handed down to you from family members, you won't keep it long if you do not have a good work ethic. This is paramount to any goal in life you wish to achieve. The path to laziness leads to destruction. People who never succeed are those who give up at the first sign of difficulty.

It's not just how hard you work, success is also about your level of energy. High energy people will always achieve greater success than lower energy people.

High energy is contagious and attracts people. How you do anything is how you do everything. If you go about achieving your goals with a ho-hum attitude, you will experience less-than-stellar results.

Luckily, if you don't have a good work ethic, you can develop it. If you are lazy by nature, plan each day to accomplish a task you would ordinarily defer and see the transformation occur as you begin to enjoy helping and serving others who are integral to the achievement of your goals. Start by doing little things today instead of putting them off until tomorrow. Practice having high energy. It's in everyone's capabilities to get pumped up about success.

5. Positive Attitude

Successful people always see the glass half full instead of half empty. And because they are positive, they tend to stay away from negative people who drain their energy. They look for the good in every situation, seeing speed bumps only as unexpected opportunities.

There's two ways you can look at the things that happen to you: negatively or positively. You can either view them as the means to destroy your life or you can view them as strengthening and empowering tools. I'm imagining you will choose the latter if success is truly your goal.

6. Discipline and Focus

Along every journey to success there will be enticing detours that attempt to steer you off course, many of them billboards with tempting promises of fun and relaxation (the beach, anyone?), good food (world's best pie) and something really cool to see (a giant ball of twine). If you are ever going to be successful, however, you must stick to the route that leads directly to your goal. Those who often get sidetracked are no doubt good at devising goals but rarely, if ever, completing them. Their motivation gets tossed from the window and they end up derailing their goals due to lack of focus.

You can bet there will be many instances when people or events step into the path of your success journey. The difference between winners and losers is that winners refuse to lose focus when presented with distractions. You must refocus on your motivations in order to stay disciplined, to keep your eyes on the ultimate goal instead of a fleeting, tempting distraction.

7. Fearless

The number one reason most of us never achieve our goals is due to fear. Fear is the main barrier on your journey to success: fear of failure, rejection, making mistakes, what other people think, loss of time or money – whatever it is you fear most, you can bet it's the biggest obstacle to your success.

The opposite of fear is courage. It takes great courage to make decisions and set goals because this means you must prove that you can follow your own goals through to a successful conclusion. It takes courage to make a real decision about something you will actually do. You will have to make sacrifices in order to fulfill your ultimate goals.

Many people do not set personal goals because they are afraid of failing. They reason that the best way to avoid defeat is to simply quit trying to attain that which they desire. You need to fall down. You need to hurt yourself. You need to take chances and you need to fail. It is only through repeated failures that you will learn the most important lessons in life.

If you are unable to conquer your fears, you will forever be stuck on the sidelines of success. You must make a conscious effort to overcome your subconscious mind, where the fear keeping you within your comfort zone resides. You must challenge your fears, conquer them, and relieve yourself of those chains. Say to yourself, "I can do this! I can be bigger than my fear!"

Now believe it – and do it. It must be your decision to overcome your fears once and for all so you quit stalling out when the unfamiliar and uncomfortable obstructs your path. Go after what you want in life and be willing to fail over and over again. Be unafraid to hurt and chances are, you will find the pain is far less than you imagined.

8. Well-defined Goals

Without a goal, it is almost impossible to know when you have achieved success. Can you imagine a large corporation starting the fiscal year with an attitude of "going with the flow", rather than having a solid plan in place? How would they know if they'd reached the end point without a plan defining where they wanted to go?

What about you? Do you have a plan for your life or do you just go wherever the tide washes you ashore? If you have this attitude, you will never achieve your goals.

The most important step for starting any business or project or dream is devising well thought out goals and putting them in writing. This way, you are held accountable to achieving those goals and you can remind yourself where you are headed when your commitment and motivation wane.

If you meditate on your goals daily, your actions will be subconsciously guided to achieve them. And if you visualize them on a regular basis, you set the power of intention and provide the motivation necessary to fuel your journey all the way to the end.

9. Self Motivation

Most people wait to take action until someone else tells them what to do. That's the way our society is organized. From the very beginning of life, your parents told you what is right and what is wrong. As a child, you went to school, where a teacher guided your learning. After high school, you may have studied at a university, where professors told you what was necessary to obtain a degree. You may have opted to join the armed services and did only what your drill sergeant told you to do. Chances are you now have a job with a boss and colleagues, all of whom tell you what to do on a daily basis.

Sure, we all have to learn from others but we do have a choice about where we get advice. If you wish to know how to establish your own business, would you ask someone who has been stuck in a regular nine-to-five job for the past several decades? If you want to become an entrepreneur, examine the habits of people who started their own companies and made them successful; find out what worked for them.

Anyone who heads his own business – or several – and achieves topnotch results, does so through sheer motivation and determination. We can only achieve success if we like what we do and if we keep doing it using the wealth of self-motivation and commitment located deep within ourselves. You may not be able to see it at all times, but it is there. It's up to you to figure out how to reach it when the fun and excitement of your new venture wears off.

10. Self Investment

When you decide to start your own business you are also deciding to go back to school again. You might never step foot in a classroom but you must be willing to learn new things.

You must dig for every single bit of information that will get you closer to your goal. Top entrepreneurs read business and marketing books, magazines, reports, journals, newsletters, websites and industry publications, knowing these resources will improve their understanding of business in general, sales and marketing in particular, and the various functions and skills necessary to create a successful company. They network with other skilled businesspeople to learn their secrets of success and help define their own personal goals and objectives. They attend business and marketing seminars, workshops and training courses, even if they believe they have already mastered the subject matter.

Successful people do this because they know that education is an ongoing process. There are always ways to do things better, in less time, with less effort. We never stop learning until the day we die. One of the best things you can improve on, in order to reach success, is to become coachable. Quit thinking you know it all because you don't! Sometimes all it takes is one little nugget of information you glean from studying someone else to make the difference between success and failure.

Top entrepreneurs never stop investing in the most powerful, effective and best business and marketing tool at their immediate disposal: their own knowledge. They invest in personal development because it makes sense; it's just one more way of reaching their goals.

11. Willingness to Change

Habits are established patterns of behavior and thinking you have acquired throughout your life. To learn something new, to obtain new knowledge and skills, requires you to change at least some of your habits.

If you wish to learn a foreign language you will do so much more easily when you make changes to your daily routine. Instead of listening to your favorite music on your iPod as you get ready each morning, you could download an audio recording in the language you are learning. It's so much easier to do what you want to do, such as indulge in a good mystery, than encourage yourself to read something less interesting but that could be really helpful in terms of goal achievement.

We all have a tendency to get used to things that are not only comfortable but that do not require much mental activity on our part. You have to change your habit of absorbing information passively into one of actively searching for information in order to analyze, filter, absorb and reorganize it. Constant learning and changing habits to align with goals are the hallmarks of successful people.

12. A System

Success usually follows a formula; it fits into a prescribed system. When you imagine some of the greatest goals possible, you are sure to identify at least one other person who has already been there, done that.

Many people shy away from using systems because they think it will limit their creativity. If that's you, try letting go of this thought and working inside a structured environment to see what benefits it provides. Thinking in unlimited terms is overwhelming. Often, we can become more creative if we put a little structure around our tasks, give ourselves boundaries by which to define the things we must do.

Some of the most successful people in the world develop systems in order to make certain their businesses and their lives are triumphant. Think of your favorite fast food restaurant, movie theatre, or retail store; they are popular because their service and products are consistent; they demand that managers and employers do things a certain way. Successful franchises work by creating a system and using it to provide consistency across owners, locations, and even cultures. McDonald's is a good example of this; when the fast food giant expanded its restaurant chain to other countries, they had to change many menu items, but they kept their system of providing high service and food quality standards the same.

You don't need to recreate the wheel in order to devise a system that works for your company. Many times there's someone who has already figured out what is necessary and they've put together a step-by-step game plan that will show you exactly how to recreate their success. Even if you feel the need to start from scratch, take what you know already works and use that to devise a system for consistently recreating success over and over again. Search online for existing formulas in your industry or type of business. Save time and stress by utilizing proven formulas – someone else's or your own.

Systems allow you to spend less time thinking about what needs to be done and more time doing the things that lead to success.

13. Bending Instead of Breaking

You will face many challenges along the road to victory. It's not that you might be put to the test, you can count on it! The difference between those who overcome and those who give up is whether they bend or break, whether they grow stronger or weaker in the face of adversity.

Consider the aptly named Lone Cypress. This amazing tree grows along the California coastline on Seventeen Mile Drive. It not only survives but thrives among some of the most difficult weather conditions you can imagine. High winds, heavy rains, and frequent storms threaten this tough little tree daily.

How does it thrive? Simple – it offers no resistance to the elements. It bends and twists to accommodate the weather conditions, all the while making itself stronger with each passing storm.

If you take two seeds and plant one in a sunny window and the other outside, the one outside will always be stronger. Why? The outdoor plant is subject to punishing wind and pounding rain. As it resists these forces, it grows a bigger, tougher stem to provide an exceptionally strong foundation. The indoor plant may have everything it needs to grow, but without these challenges it will reach for the light with a slender, easily damaged stalk. Do you keep yourself protected? You can't be an overcomer without facing challenges you're forced to overcome.

Whatever happens in your life, learn to reroute your path so you go with the wind instead of fighting to go the opposite direction. Try to bend instead of break, and when you can't, confront your challenges head on and strengthen from the unexpected experience.

These thirteen attributes of highly successful people present wonderful opportunities to create personal goals that allow you to grow. But remember, it's not always that easy. You can expect challenges and even failure in your quest for success. It is not that successful people do not fail; instead they decide to fail forward rather than fall backward and quit. When you learn to fail forward, failures no longer bother you and, in fact, through failure you become a stronger person.

Wondering how to fail forward? Here are a few of the things that successful people always do. Why not learn from their journeys?

Learn From Failure

Why do we fail? Simply because we have not taken the right fork in the road, somewhere along the journey to success. Perhaps there is something in us lacking fortitude or wisdom, or we do not know the right way to perform necessary tasks. So we fail.

It is better to make a wrong decision and fall short rather than not take any action at all. So, make an action plan using whatever information you have available and perform it to the best of your ability. Do not wait until you have a foolproof plan in place, because there is no such thing. Make a plan and take action now.

When you take action two things can happen; either you succeed or you fail. If you succeed the first time (which is unlikely, but possible), then congratulations! But if you fail, sit back and analyze why. You don't know what you don't know. Every failure adds to your life experience; you come away with the knowledge of one more way that something should not be done. As a result you will be able to make a better plan next time.

When one plan doesn't work, again, take action and create a new plan. The same two results can happen: success or failure. If that doesn't work, go through the same process a third time and a fourth, and keep on trying until you succeed. After analysis of your failure, determine the skills you are lacking and then take the action of acquiring them.

Learn to Say, "Next"

Rejection is a part of life. There is no one in this world who has never been rejected. There is no one who has never failed. You don't need to mourn either failure or rejection. Life is too short to call it quits every time something doesn't go as planned. So, what do you do? Simply say "Next!" and move on.

Next is a powerful word. It makes you look forward into the future; it fills you with hope and fresh, positive aspirations.

When you complete your quota for failure, all you are left with is success. So keep trying and keep taking risks until you are done with failure. The "next" time is when you will achieve success.

Analyze Success

So far I have told you only to analyze your failures, since they will give you important information about what you lack and an opportunity to improve yourself. But when you really decide to fail forward, you must also analyze your successes.

Every time you fail, think of the times you succeeded – and don't think there are none because it would be impossible that you do not have even a single success in your past experience. It could be as small as getting a good grade in middle school or as significant as landing a major client while working for a big corporation. Think about those instances and use them to create a success list.

Now, analyze what you did to bring about those successes. If you examine the details of them all, large and small, you will soon realize what works for you. Just add that ingredient to your goal-achieving plan and see how quickly your results change for the better.

If success is what you want, do not get obsessed with the vehicle you are driving to reach that goal. One vehicle is the profession you choose. Most people work at a particular profession because they feel it can lead to success faster. But that seldom happens. After a time, they become disillusioned and see themselves going somewhere they do not want to go – or going nowhere at all. Still, they remain stuck in the same job year after year, and wish things would change, somehow, some way.

How can you get out of a rut? The answer is very simple. The definition of insanity is continuing to do the same thing while expecting different results. If the vehicle you are presently driving on the path to success is stalling out along the way, dare to trade it in for a new one. Dare to set a new course. Yes, change is difficult, but change also means growth, and so it is worth the possibility of failure in order to achieve it.

8 Reasons Why You Should Never Give Up

Do you still need the motivation and courage to get the car out of the garage and point your wheels down the road to success?

At some point in our journey we arrive at a treacherous section of the route where it seems easiest to just give up. Sometimes we give up before we even start, and other times we give up just before we are about to make it over that huge hump obstructing the path. Take a deep breath and review these eight things to help you start down the path to success – or to get back on the smooth track.

1. Realistically Speaking, You Will Make Mistakes

The chance of mastering something the first time you do it is almost non-existent. Everything takes time to learn and you will make mistakes. The difference between a winner and a loser is learning from missteps.

There are many famous people who have made big mistakes and made them publicly. But they didn't give up; instead they strengthened and matured from the experience.

Consider Lance Armstrong. Armstrong was diagnosed with serious cancer that had spread throughout his entire body. He had cancer cells the size of golf balls in his lungs. Despite all odds, he overcame the cancer and set out to regain the top ranking in his sport. He went on to win the Tour de

France six consecutive years in a row after being diagnosed with cancer.

Muhammad Ali was one of the best boxers the world has ever known; he suffered only five losses while earning fifty-six wins in the ring and was the first boxer to win the Heavyweight Championship of the World title three times. This is a guy who literally knows how to get knocked down and get back up.

Use these examples of famous people to provide the motivation you need to keep moving forward and learn from the mistakes you are bound to experience. If they can do it, so can you!

2. *Prove to Yourself That You Can Do It*

You don't want to be known as someone who is weak and gives up easily. Go out there and prove yourself to the world – and to yourself. You can and will achieve what you set out to do. The only time you fail is when you give up.

3. Ask if it's Been Done Before

If someone else can do what you are setting out to do, then so can you. Even if there is only one other person in the world who has achieved the goal you've set for yourself, that should be reason enough for you to never give up.

4. Believe in Your Dreams

Don't sell yourself short. In life there are always many people who will try to bring you down and tell you what you want to achieve is not possible. Don't let anyone destroy your dreams.

5. You Can Improve the World

When you achieve whatever you set out to do, you can use your success to make a difference in other people's lives. It could be that while developing a new product, you discover the next medical miracle. Maybe in the course of starting your own business you use the opportunity to hire a handicapped person. Now aren't those worthwhile goals?

6. Let the Haters Hate

There will always be haters – those people who just can't find it within themselves to offer you a pat on the back when they witness your success. There will always be plenty of negative people trying to tear you down. Don't pay attention to them and don't take what they say to heart. Let the haters hate while you continue believing in yourself. Keep that mindset and never give up until you find your success!

7. Inspire Others to be Successful, Too

Be an inspiration to others by refusing to give up. Who knows what someone else will achieve because they witnessed the fact that you never gave up. Wouldn't it feel great to provide inspiration to someone who needs a little extra motivation to succeed?

8. Don't Stop When You Are So Close

We tend to reach our breaking point just when we are closest to making a breakthrough. Remember this when you feel like you want to give up. At any given time you are undoubtedly just a heartbeat away from success. Would you really risk everything you've worked so hard to achieve just because you got a bit tired?

I urge you to quit worrying about whether or not you've got enough fuel in your tank to make it all the way down the path to success. Quit fearing failure. Quit worrying about making a mistake. Just get in the car, put it in Drive, and get it out of the garage!

EXERCISE: Standing Up to Naysayers

When you begin to implement your dream and make it come to life you are bound to encounter those who will try their best to sabotage it. Even your closest friends and family members can unwittingly put a wrench in the works through their words and actions. Some people have probably already done this to you in the past and said things like:

- "You can't do this."
- "You don't have what it takes."
- "That's too hard…just give up now."
- "This is a scam! It's a pyramid scheme!"
- "You are so selfish for doing this."
- "This is ridiculous. People will laugh at you."
- "You will lose the respect of everyone if you do this."

Take a piece of paper right now and write down three to five things you expect people will say to you to quash your willingness to succeed.

Look in the mirror and pretend you are facing one of those people in person. Say to them in a very loud voice (yes, go ahead and say each of these phrases out loud):

- "Thank you for sharing but I have a "WHATEVER IT TAKES ATTITUDE" and I will not give up."
- "Thank you for sharing but I have a "NO QUIT ATTITUDE" and I will not give up."
- "Thank you for sharing but I have the STAYING POWER to achieve my goals.

Now you have a plan for dealing with the intended or unintended sabotage of your friends and family members. That's something to celebrate!

Chapter Five:
That Voice in Your Head is Giving You the Wrong Directions

> *"If you hear a voice within you say 'you cannot paint,' then by all means paint, and that voice will be silenced."*
> – Vincent Van Gogh

I like to think all human beings are born with a personalized GPS system that comes with its own disembodied voice giving us directions. You may refer to this as your "little voice", that inner dialogue that occurs in your head at any given moment. While it can provide support for the goals you are trying to achieve, most often it will do just the opposite by convincing you to stop trying.

Your little voice has probably talked to you thousands of time. Even today it might have already told you things such as:

- "Why are you reading this book right now? It's not going to do you any good. You won't use this information any more than the last self-help book you read."

- "I can't believe what I said during dinner last night. What must my friends think of me?"

- "I need to read more of this stuff because I'm such a loser."

- "I really don't want to go to work tomorrow. I wonder if I can call in sick again."

Honestly, our little voices have thousands of things to tell us each and every day. They don't ever stop talking and they are very good at trash talk. If we aren't careful, they can run our lives by dictating what we do and how we feel about ourselves.

You already know that mastering the little voice in your head is one of those roadblocks to success you must overcome, right? Thanks for Blair Singer, author of the book, *Little Voice Mastery*, I've summarized the top methods for taking control of your little voice. So here are thirteen "how to" methods of doing just that.

1. How to Handle Success

How many times have you achieved success at something, anything, only to hear your little voice chime in and discount your victory? Next time that happens, take a minute to stop and think about these very simple but powerful techniques that use physical and verbal gestures to squelch your inner voice and allow you to celebrate success:

- If something good happens and your little voice wants to discount it, say out loud, and with force, "Stop!"
- Don't let your little voice tell you "Oh, I was just lucky" or "I don't know why this good thing happened to me…just luck I guess." Stop and say, "I deserve it, the power of intention sent it to me."
- You must celebrate your successes. When you have success, tell yourself the rest of the week will be great. With your right hand, make a fist and say "Yes!"

So take that win and project that positive energy back onto yourself. Remember that the highest energy always wins. You deserve success – so celebrate your victories, however small!

2. How to Handle Adversity

Most people fear rejection. That's perfectly natural. But as we've already considered, it's a sure thing you will encounter rejection so it's important to know how to handle it.

If someone rejects you, says no to you, or acts in a way you perceive to be negative, don't take it personally. What you say to yourself in the first minute after this happens is vital.

Don't allow your little voice to say something negative, as "This doesn't work", "I can't do this", "This is crap", "I'm not cut out for this". Never allow the rejection to be globalized and think such things as, "The same thing happens to me at work, at home, with friends, etc." Don't protract this negative emotion to other areas of your life. If you want to say negative things to yourself, say "Stop!" and instead, focus on a positive statement such as:

- "The customer didn't buy from me today but I got her to agree to an appointment next week. I'll wow her my presentation then!"
- "I'll have another opportunity tomorrow to make someone's day."
- "I'm going to set aside time tomorrow for a brainstorming session to figure out a creative way to sidestep this problem."

Repeat positive statements such as these three to four times and feel your energy increase, circulating positive emotions throughout your body.

It is critical to master this technique. Do not allow rejection to fester for even a few seconds after it occurs. This negative energy is difficult to overcome and can really sidetrack you from your achievements. You must build on every single accomplishment in order to achieve monumental success. By the same token, if you allow every rejection to infuse negative emotions into your thoughts, actions, and words, you will build a foundation of pessimism that grows even larger and more detrimental over time.

3. How to React to Fear

If something drives a knot in your stomach or makes sweat pour down your back, there's a good chance it is a situation that you have been programmed to fear. We've already examined ways to overcome fear but there are certain things, such as approaching a co-worker to discuss a highly personal subject, going on a blind date, or having a sticky conversation with your spouse, that don't happen often. And when they do, we instinctively react with dread. Even more everyday situations, like asking someone for payment or the prospect of making a presentation to a room full of strangers could elicit the same anxious response.

This is prime time for your little voice to pipe up and remind you, "I don't want to look like an idiot."

If you think the worst will happen, it will.

When your fear response kicks into high gear, think of a previous time when you succeeded at doing something really awesome. Take your right hand, make a fist and say "Yes!" This reminds you of all the successes you've had in the past, promoting positive energy.

4. How to Debrief Yourself

Whenever you experience something that elicits strong emotion – whether positive or negative, a win or a loss – you will need to calm yourself down afterward. Otherwise your little voice will have a heyday, preying on your emotions and getting you hyped up even more. Your job is to manage these incidences before they manage you.

Ask yourself a series of questions:
- "What happened?"
- "What went right?"
- "What didn't work?"
- "Why did that happen?"
- "How can I make that happen again?"

OR
- "How can I avoid that in the future?"

Let's say that you were making a presentation to a client and things went terribly wrong, causing you deep despair and feelings of anxiety. Look for patterns of behavior and examine the experience. You might answer those questions like this:

- "What happened?"
  - "The client was uncomfortable about price."
- "What did I learn?"
  - "I learned that I need to try a different presentation with new pricing options or to use different vocabulary that sounds more positive."
- "What did you learn about you?"
  - "I get nervous and my palms get sweaty when I talk about pricing with a customer."

This question and answer process allows you to go back in the past and figure out things to do differently, in order to achieve a better outcome. You can also determine what you did right in order to replicate that success again next time you encounter the same situation. The idea is to take the incident and figure out all the variables so you know the right formula and have nothing to fear when it happens again in the future.

5. How to Celebrate All Wins

Much like handling success, it's important that you have a physical way to celebrate all of your victories and cement them in your subconscious. Remember that over time you are reprogramming yourself and teaching your little voice how to respond in a positive way each time something good happens. Your body will remember your celebration gesture, such as giving yourself a high five, doing a fist pump, or even giving yourself a pat on the back (literally).

Your body is like a computer and it will remember those previous successes, associating them with the fist pump that promotes positive emotion. If you want to stockpile even more positive, high energy, celebrate other people's wins as well as your own. They will appreciate you and you will benefit through an infusion of upbeat power that fills the room.

6. How to Set Goals

Ssh...I'm going to tell you a secret about setting goals; a technique few people know about or understand. Even if you've read a lot about the best way to handle goals, you've probably never heard about this one.

However, there's a caveat: if you don't handle this technique properly, it can cause you to crash and burn. You may even lower your expectations because you base it on your past goal performance.

Let's take a for instance...if last year's income goal for yourself was to make $100,000 and you only earned $90,000, you probably consider this a failure; after all you didn't meet your goal. And because you failed this time, you will lower that amount when you set your goal for the upcoming year.

That's not a good idea.

Due to human nature, you could be tempted to give up on goals in the future because you feel as if you are setting yourself up for failure. After all, you might reason, if I can't achieve the goal, what's the point of establishing it in the first place?

Rather than focusing on the negative (failure to completely achieve the goal), you need to instead examine all the other aspects of your performance. Sit down and discuss what happened with someone you trust (or record your voice talking it out, if no one else is available). Reiterate the projected goal and recount what you actually did accomplish. List everything positive that happened on the way to the goal. For instance, you might not have earned $100,000 but maybe you were able to afford a new car, take a training class and learn new insights into your profession, or accrue more vacation time that you spent with your family.

Listen closely and determine which of those positive things you react to with the most energy. Which makes your tone of voice go up and your energy level to rise?

The lesson here? You just might discover that the goal you set out to achieve was not the real goal. Sometimes achieving an underlying goal can represent a bigger win.

As you talk about your journey toward making $100,00 last year, you just might realize that what you really wanted was the respect and recognition of your spouse or your boss. The amount of money earned really didn't matter.

Follow the road you took to attempt to reach that last goal and look back at what you actually achieved. That is more important and often more therapeutic, because it reveals what you really want – and may even redefine what you view as real success.

When you set a goal and it doesn't happen, list what you did that was great. The next goal will be bigger and better (not smaller and lesser because you fear failure). There is no such thing as total failure; you have the opportunity to learn something from every experience, good or bad, not the least of which is how to silence the little voice inside that says you cannot achieve big goals so why even try?

7. How to Overcome the Fear of Making Mistakes

As a general rule, the biggest fear most people have is of public humiliation. The fear of looking stupid, however, is a great hindrance to success and one of the most important roadblocks to overcome. This is the number one reason that people prevent themselves from getting what they want in life.

Fear is a critical factor in sales and particularly in speaking on stage. You might think that you are not directly involved in sales so this doesn't apply to you. But just imagine...what kind of business is there where you don't have to sell something – whether a product, a service, or even yourself? Sales is truly a part of any venture and always a task at which the successful entrepreneur must succeed.

The best way to get over the fear of looking silly or humiliating yourself in front of others is to celebrate your mistakes. Yep, the same way you celebrate your successes works equally as well for celebrating mistakes: make a fist with one hand and say "Yes!"

Do this anytime you have stage fright, anytime you feel intimidated, anytime you are afraid of looking stupid, anytime you feel something you are doing isn't going to work. Override your fear with celebration. In this way you are reprogramming how you think about making mistakes or looking stupid. When you make the process of muffling your little voice fun, you will be much more willing to jump on stage and accept any dare that comes your way.

8. How to be Present

When you are with someone else, how often are you really in the moment? Out of 7 billion people on this earth, I would estimate that 6.9 billion of them are not able to be present, right here and right now in this moment. But this is extremely important in order to connect with others – and if you can't make that connection, your chances of achieving what you desire drop drastically.

We've all had experiences where we have been in the company of someone who really isn't present – a person who is physically there but not mentally connected. You talk to them but it's apparent in their eyes or gestures that they are a million miles away, planning their next day off or considering which restaurant sounds best for dinner. How does that make you feel?

Now imagine if you are doing the same thing to a customer, or your boss, or your spouse. Don't they deserve your full attention, in the here and now?

Try this exercise. Look at yourself in a mirror. Don't talk, don't flinch, and don't blink – for at least three minutes. Let your little voice say what it will but stay in the moment. Listen to it say things like, "This is stupid", "When are three minutes going to be up?", "What is that little bump on the side of my nose?" It's okay to let your little voice continue its dialogue. Eventually you will find peace. Even as you listen to yourself, you will connect with the person in the mirror.

Use this activity when you are feeling scattered, when your thoughts are running every which way and refuse to be calmed. Refocus and bring yourself back to the present, on an hourly basis, if necessary.

When you are present in the here and now, other people will naturally be attracted to you. They will want to be in your company. Doesn't that sound good? How could you use that to your benefit?

9. How to Anchor Love

What's even more powerful than success? The answer is love.

When your day is going completely wrong or life in general just seems tougher than it should, all you need to do is go back to a moment in your past when you felt comforted by love, when you felt unequivocally, one hundred percent loved, cherished and wanted. That love might have come from a parent or a spouse or a child – it doesn't matter. What does matter are the feelings of comfort and joy you recall as a result of experiencing the strong, positive emotion of love.

Right now, take a moment to go back and time and recall that situation, exactly what you saw, what you felt, what was being said. Really anchor that memory of love, whether it comes from the birth of your child, your wedding day, a romantic outing, or a time when your mother comforted you.

When you can feel it and see it and experience it fully, make a fist with your right hand and say "Yes!"

Anytime you are nervous or intimidated or face a difficult task, bring back this memory and make it your love anchor. Use it to provide the instant strength to accomplish what you must. Evoke the positive emotion and feel it course through your body, providing deep strength to face whatever the rest of your day may bring.

10. How to Brag

Chances are you've been taught that it's wrong to brag. We are supposed to be humble, not toot our own horns. But there really is a time and place when bragging is important; you can use it to bolster your self image.

It could be that you avoid looking good in front of others because you don't want to be humiliated when you can't live up to the higher standard you've publicly set for yourself.

Sometimes boasting is just what we need to get past a difficult roadblock and develop real confidence. It is a great way to help you feel good about life in general, particularly when everything seems so miserable.

Remember that your little voice is always there to put down your efforts, but now you are retraining it to lift yourself up. It's a game you play with your brain to turn self-doubt into confidence. So go ahead and brag! Everyone deserves a moment in the spotlight to bask in the glory of doing something right.

11. How to Clean Up Justifications

Just when you are at the lowest point, when your little voice plants seeds of doubt about your abilities, is when you examine your life and come up with a list of shortfalls. Your subconscious will imagine what you should have done, could have done and would have done, with a list of justifications at the ready, rather than owning up to the mistake.

For example, you might be lying in bed at night while your mind races about how you should have gone to the gym before coming home, how you could have made more sales at work today and how you should have called your mother-in-law to ask her how she's feeling after recovering from an illness. But you didn't accomplish these things because you had other obligations, you were tired, you forgot, you didn't make time, etc.

Rather than agonizing and losing sleep over all this mental garbage, add all the missed opportunities and justifications to a written list. Read through them over and over again until you finally find the humor in the situation. You didn't make time? *Ha! That's a good one!* When could you have managed to do that along with taking the kids to soccer practice, making dinner, and reviewing those month-end reports from work? Let the guilt go with a laugh and cleanse it from your system once and for all.

Use this magical tool to clean up the little voice in your brain. Tomorrow is another day; use it more wisely, but forget about today because it is in the past.

12. How to Ask Yourself

There are many things that derail our best efforts to move forward toward our goals. One of the nastiest is when your little voice says those two words we all dread, "I can't." This often happens when you are overwhelmed by life, when things just seem to be careening out of control.

Stop paying attention to negativity. It's all in your head!

Never let your little voice be the roadblock to success. "I can't" really means "I don't want to."

When you catch your inner voice being a naysayer, stop it right away. Say, "Stop!" out loud.

Once you stop the chatter there are two options. First, you can continue with the thought that you can't... and then lie or exaggerate wildly about the reasons why. Tell yourself, "I can't do it because my shirt is blue" or "I can't do this because my eyes are green." Make the reasons ridiculous and keep at it until you laugh or become bored with the process.

Then remind yourself of all the things you can do, even little things like, "I can brush my teeth", "I can walk", or "I can tie my shoes." Ask yourself, "If I could do this one thing I am dreading but I know needs to get done, what would be the first step I would take?"

Odds are good that you are projecting negative thoughts because you simply don't want to do what needs to be accomplished. Ask yourself why. It's important to get to the emotional truth in order to find out what's really going on inside your head and overcome these subconscious efforts to sabotage your dreams.

13. How to Learn What You Need to

There are going to be roadblocks and pitfalls and detours on your journey to success. Chances are, when you are faced with new challenges or risks, your little voice will respond by telling you to bail out. Ditch your dreams. Quit moving forward and stay where you are because it's comfortable right here, right now.

We tend to cruise along until we get to the border of unknown territory, to the edge of fear and risk. That's a scary place. Your little voice is sure to pipe up and remind you that you don't know how to proceed or make you wonder if you should even bother trying.

The easy thing to say to yourself is, "I don't know how". In this way you surrender your power to someone else, some divine, otherworldly entity who can control your fate so you don't have to make a decision that might be wrong.

You could take the higher road and ask for the information you need. Unfortunately, less than 5 percent of us will actually apply the good advice we receive and continue our journey. The other 95 percent listen to their little voices and convince themselves they aren't cut out for this particular success goal while justifying why they shouldn't continue the journey.

When this little voice pops up, you say, "Stop!"

Now refer back to #11, "How to Clean Up Justifications" and make up silly stories about the reasons why you can't accomplish that which you need to do, "I don't know how because pianos have benches", "I can't because pink elephants fly." Tell stories boldly about your justifications until you get bored with this exercise, then focus on what you can do.

Ask yourself this out loud, "What do I know how to do?" Your energy will rise as you recount all the things you can do, and do well, however trivial.

When you can master these techniques for quelling that inner voice using words like "no", "can't", "don't", "fear" and "shouldn't", you will be well on your way to forging a new path for your life that heads straight for success. You can control your mind and reprogram its GPS to take the right road, even if it is fraught with forks and potholes and speed bumps. The journey is worth it; convince your mind of that and success will happen as a result.

To learn even more about mastering the little voice in your head, please refer to Blair Singer's fantastic book, *Little Voice Mastery*. It's a great read for anyone who is particularly challenged by negative inner dialogue.

EXERCISE: Boast About Yourself

This exercise can takes seconds or minutes, depending how far you want to take it – and how far down in the dumps you are feeling.

All you are going to do is brag; boast about yourself in big, bold, loud proportions. Become a legend in your own mind for at least one minute.

Talk as loudly as you can. Stand on a chair or a table and proclaim your assets. Say things like:

- "I'm the greatest person on the planet."
- "When people encounter me, they just can't walk away."
- "I am irresistible to others."
- "I the greatest lover ever."
- "I am so hot people can barely touch me."
- "My future is so bright, I've got to wear shades."

Rant and rave about how great you are! You don't even have to brag about something big, a simple, "I made it to work on time this morning!" can be just fine.

Does this sound silly, crazy, or delusional? Your little voice is probably saying, "I can't do this!" or "This is stupid!"

Do it anyway, because two things will happen. For one, your energy will rise. For another, you will believe your words, whether or not they are true. Give the little voice in your brain the notion that you are great and that you can do great things. It will help you make a connection to success, to remind you of actual things you have done well.

It's perfectly fine to boost yourself through boasting – and it does wonders for your self esteem.

Chapter Six:
Decide on Success with the Power of Intention

> *"I may err in judgment, but I hope not in intention."* – Edward Blake

Have you ever felt like all the forces in the universe were working against you – that everyone and everything was working together to ensure you would never reach your goals? What if you could learn to harness all that energy and turn it around into a positive force that actually supports your goals? Wouldn't that be a powerful way to separate yourself from those who just dream but never do?

Luckily you *can* use that force. It's called the power of intention and it works through you.

When you embrace this force and let it do its magic rather than fighting the intent, you will soon realize that everything begins with a source of energy that is not only within you, but available throughout the universe – yours for the taking!

Intention is not something you do but something you connect to. You see, you are already connected to intention. However, you may have a difficult time using it to support your journey to success because you are not making a conscious effort to harness its power.

How do you do that? Here's the secret: you don't attract what you want; you attract what you are. So if you are negative, you will attract the negative energy of everything and everyone around you. It stands to reason, then, that those who focus on being positive will attract all that is good. Unfortunately, It's not quite that simple.

The power of intention is a positive force. It is harnessed in teachings of forgiveness, kindness, and love. It does not teach wanting or greed.

The notion of seeking what you want, or think you need, is not what the power of intention is all about. That type of energy belongs to the ego. The ego's mantra is, "What's in it for me? How can I get more?" It's your ego, your false self, that selfishly wants a BMW in your driveway next Thursday. The ego is what we call the false self.

Think of the power of intention as an electrical connection fueling your journey to success. There is a frequency of energy that manifests itself through the process of giving, of allowing, of offering and of serving. It is given freely and asks nothing in return. Unlike gasoline, the cost doesn't go up and there is no shortage.

If such a free source of ultimate power were available, why wouldn't you use it to reach your goals? The only reason would be ignorance. Let's consider how and where you can find and use the power of intention.

Deciding is the First Step

In order to connect to your intentions, you must use the power of intention as it was meant to be used. This allows you to make good decisions that are not based on selfish desires.

The power of intention is harnessed when you decide you are going to do something, no other reasoning than that! If it's for the greater good of all, than what you are seeking will manifest itself, and if not, then it won't. But the first step is always to decide.

Goal achievement is like the cause and effect of the power of intention. Your goals is the effect, the cause is the decision to attain it. Sounds simple enough, right?

Allow me to use a common example to better illustrate how the power of intention starts with the decision-making process.

If your goal is to make dinner, then you might think the cause (of dinner) would be the series of preparation steps, e.g. shopping for the ingredients necessary for the dishes you wish to prepare, heating them up in a pan or putting a dish into the oven, spooning it onto a plate, etc. This is an "action-reaction" level of goal attainment. You take the necessary steps and voila! Your goal is attained!

To an outside observer, that certainly appears to be the case. The scientific method would suggest that this is how things work, based on a purely objective observation. The end result you desire is dinner; in order to achieve that you must actually put food together and present it on a plate.

But first you must *decide* to make dinner and *decide* what you are going to prepare before you can *decide* to go shopping and assemble ingredients. The steps involved are not really the cause. The actions themselves are an effect; they represent the way a particular result is obtained.

What's the real cause? The real cause is the decision you made to create that effect in the first place. That's the moment you said to yourself, "Let it be" or "make it so."

At some point you decided to make dinner. That decision may have been subconscious, but it was still a decision. Without that decision dinner would never manifest itself. That decision ultimately caused the whole series of actions necessary to make it happen and finally, the manifestation of your dinner. This is referred to as an "intention-manifestation" model of goal attainment.

If you want to achieve a goal you've set, the most crucial part is to decide to manifest it; in other words you must nurture the right mindset and then set off on a course for a particular destination. It doesn't matter if you feel it's outside your control to actually reach the end. It doesn't matter if you can't yet see the path from point A to B. Most of those resources will come into existence after you've made the decision, not beforehand.

If you don't understand this simple step, then you will waste a lot of time. Step one is to decide, always. Not to ruminate or ponder or ask around and determine whether or not you can actually do it. If you want to be financially free, then decide to make it so. If you want to be married and have a family, then decide to attract a mate. If you want to change careers, then decide to find a new job.

Working With the Universe Toward Any Goal

It is mind boggling to think that people assume something else has to come before they make a decision. They waste months trying to figure out, "Is this goal possible?" But all they are really doing is creating a delay, and they will simply manifest evidence to suggest that the goal is both possible and not possible. You think doubt in your head, you will find doubt in the world. Remember confirmation bias? Your mind will think and think until it comes up with excuses that fit into your negative belief system.

The universe, itself, can sense a lack of commitment to a goal. Have you ever had a friend tell you about a goal of theirs in a very timid way? Could you easily sense just how wishy-washy and uncertain she was about it? She might have said something like, "Well, I'm going to try this new business venture and see how it goes. Hopefully it will work out okay." Is that evidence that a clear decision has been made? Not remotely. Are you going to help this person? Probably not — who wants to waste their time and money on someone who isn't totally committed to making it work?

But what happens when you sense total certainty in the other person? Will you help them if they ask for it? You are far more likely to offer aid to a committed person because you can tell they're eventually going to succeed and you want to be part of that success. You even feel more energized and motivated yourself, to contribute to the success of people who are very clearly committed to a goal that resonates with you and which is genuinely for the greatest good of all.

The universe, itself, works on the same principle. Think of it as the super-conscious mind. When you've made a clear, committed decision, it will open the floodgates of universal power, bringing you all the resources you need, sometimes in seemingly mysterious or impossible ways.

Do not ask the universe for what you want. Declare it. It is like planting a seed in the ground.

You do not say to the ground, "Here is the seed. Please, can you make it grow?" You simply plant the seed, and it will grow as a natural consequence of you placing it in the soil and tending to it. It is the same with your intentions. Simply plant them. There's no need to beg.

Whenever you want to set a new goal for yourself, start by setting it; make a decision about what you will work toward. Take the time to become clear about what you want, then just declare it. Say to the universe, "This is my goal. Make it so."

Make the decision first and everything else necessary – money, human resources, location, etc. – will follow. Don't second-guess intention. Everything will happen as it is supposed to, in its own time, of its own will. You can't rush it and you can't force it.

Your intention must be that your goal manifests itself in a manner that is for the greatest good of all. This is very important, as intentions that are created out of fear or greed will backfire. Intentions that are genuinely made for your own good and the best interest of all, will tend to manifest in a positive way. When your heart is pure, it will happen.

After learning about the power of intention, I've been able to use it time and time again. After I declare my intention, I wait for the resources to arrive and synchronicity to occur. Usually they begin to manifest in twenty-four to forty-eight hours, sometimes sooner. Sometimes these synchronicities appear to be the result of subconscious action. I just happen to notice things that may have been there all along, but now I see them in a new light, and they become valuable resources that I never noticed until after declaring my intention.

It wasn't very long ago that I decided to start a new business outside of my chiropractic practice.

I started, of course, by making the decision to start a new venture.

In this instance, there were three people with whom I really wanted to reconnect because I knew my new business would make a huge, positive difference in their lives, and that they would be able to help me bring it about. I hadn't been in contact with these three people in quite some time; in fact it had been years since I had talked to any of them. Of course, I couldn't just call them up randomly and say, "Hey, would you like to help me start a new business?" What I could do is set the intention which I did by asking for help and then saying out loud, "Make it so."

In less than one week, all three of those people contacted me. The first person emailed me to ask me for a favor, which once again opened up the lines of communication between us and allowed me to broach the subject of my new business in response. The second person called to wish me a happy birthday. The third person sent photos via email that had reminded him of me. Was this set of circumstances purely a coincidence? A miracle? Or had I harnessed the power of intention that flows through the universe?

I trust my intentions completely. If a goal I've set doesn't materialize, then I know it's for my own good; the universe has something else in mind for me, a greater, positive impact on the largest number of people.

It took me a number of years to completely trust this approach before I could begin to use it as my default manner of goal achievement. But now that I've learned how to harness the power of intention, I know that I can achieve anything, as long as I do it with a pure heart, in a way that benefits others.

Now that I've shared this huge advantage with you, there's no reason why you can't achieve any goal you desire, too. But so often I witness acquaintances interfering with their own goals because they do not understand the power of intention.

Most people have been taught to achieve goals on the level of action-reaction, meaning that they are purely focused on the action steps involved in getting from Point A to Point B. This goes against the laws of the universe, which see that you are putting out thoughts that conflict with the higher level of intention-manifestation. In effect, you are sabotaging yourself because you haven't made a decision or declared a goal. A goal with action is not enough, you need to create the intention!

If you go on a diet and exercise like crazy, all the while thinking, "I'm fat. This is hopeless. This is taking too long," then your higher level intentions will override your actions, and negative or incongruent results will follow.

Realize that every thought is truly an intention; *every* thought. Most people manifest a cluttered mish-mash of conflict in their lives because their thoughts are also in disarray. They simultaneously set a goal and then unset it through their subconscious thoughts and conscious actions. A statement of, "I want to start my own business" is often followed by a thought of, "I wonder if it will work" or, "Maybe my family is right, and this is a mistake." Mildly negative thoughts like "I wonder if I'll succeed" or "Maybe this won't work" quickly turn into "No, I'm pretty sure I can't succeed."

If you want to achieve a goal, you must clear out all the "hopefully" and "maybe" and "can't" nonsense from your consciousness. You cannot allow yourself the luxury of a negative thought; that is an intention to manifest exactly the opposite of what you truly desire. This takes practice of course, but it is an essential skill to learn how to use your consciousness to create what you want. When you are congruent in your thoughts, your goal will come about with greater ease. But when you are incongruent with your thoughts, you will face conflict and obstacles.

Why are you able to use the power of intention to achieve your goals? Because you have that power; it resides within you, right here and right now. Not believing in yourself simply means you are using your own power against your desires. If you think about or intend weakness, you manifest weakness.

You don't need anyone's permission to do this. It is a natural human ability. But it takes practice to develop your consciousness to the level where you can apply it and especially to learn to trust it.

So what is your goal? Say it out loud right now, and let it be the most beneficial for all. Then declare to the universe, "Make it so." Wait for the synchronicities and unusual coincidences to arrive. Follow them where they lead you, even if the destination seems strange at first. Allow your goal to manifest without interfering in the process.

The following exercise will help you use the power of intention to create the life you want, personally or professionally. Start with some simple and easy things and then work your way up to bigger, more challenging desires. As you practice using intention, be willing to see coincidences for what they are: meaningful occurrences. It is important to be open and ready for opportunities and possibilities. Let your actions be guided by your intuition and hunches. Mastering the power of intention while detaching from the outcome is the key to creating greater health, wealth, happiness, and success in your life.

EXERCISE: 8 Steps for Harnessing the Power of Intention to Achieve Goals

Are you ready to use the power of intention to attract greatness? Take the time to perform these eight steps and then watch it happen!

1. Create a Sacred Space

Creating a sacred space boosts the power of your intention. Research shows that when a particular place is used repeatedly for intention exercises, the intentions begin to "condition" the place. The space begins to hold a positive energy and that powers your intentions.

You can create a sacred space in a room in your home, a corner of your office, or even a space in your mind's eye. The important part is to use this space regularly.

Fill your sacred space with meaningful items such as mementos from a vacation, precious photos, religious items, candles, or music. Remember it is a special place for you, so use your imagination and decorate it in a way that makes you feel good.

2. Create your Intention

What is your intention? State it in a positive way, including the specific things you want, using present tense. For example, rather than saying "I will stop eating sweet foods," you will say, "I choose healthy foods that nourish my body."

The problem with the first example is that in order to think about eliminating sugary treats, you must first think about the sweets. In other words, you are keeping your mind focused on the very thing you wish to stop. In the second example, your mind focuses on healthy foods and this will lead to success in achieving your goal.

3. Get Centered

Centering is the practice of quieting the mind and relaxing the body to create a **sense of peace and** acceptance. It is a process of clearing away the mental clutter so you can access your inner resources and power, much like meditation.

Deep diaphragmatic breathing is a simple way to get centered. Place one hand on your chest and one on your abdomen and breathe naturally. Notice which hand moves more as you breathe. It is likely that the hand on your chest moves up and down more than the one on your abdomen. This indicates shallow chest breathing.

It is easy to retrain your body to breathe deeply. Imagine a balloon in your stomach. As you inhale, imagine filling this balloon up with air; your abdomen will rise. Then imagine letting the air out of this balloon as you exhale; your abdomen will deflate. Try breathing in this deep way for several minutes at a time. **Research shows** that diaphragmatic breathing produces a relaxation response. This also helps to focus and quiet your mind.

As you are centering, you will likely find that your mind wanders occasionally (there's that little voice again!). That is perfectly natural. Simply bring your awareness gently back to the quiet, peaceful mental place you've created every time you catch your little voice interfering.

4. Field of Infinite Possibilities

Once you are centered, bring your intention into your awareness. Imagine placing this intention in the field of infinite possibilities, that omniscient presence you may call God, the Universe, Spirit, or whatever aligns with your beliefs. This field of infinite possibilities is the source of all creative forces. It is where life begins and ends. It is the source of mystery, magic, and miracles.

5. Mental Rehearsal

Mental rehearsal is a powerful tool to tap into the power of intention. This process requires you to engage all of your senses to create a vivid experience in your mind's eye. Imagine yourself already having what you want to create. Mental rehearsal brings together the power of your mind with the creative power of the Universe to help you achieve your goals.

6. Banish Doubt

It is necessary to banish all doubt about whether or not you will be able to attain your goals. Trust that you will know the right steps to take and be led to the right people and opportunities to help you turn your dreams into reality. Trust that the field of infinite possibilities has unlimited organizing and creative powers that will work with you to reach your goals. Trust the power of intention.

7. Detach From the Outcome

You must detach yourself from the possible outcomes that result in obtaining your goal, and let go of the need to control the process. It will unfold in the right time and in the perfect way (remember, you must trust this will occur!). When you plant seeds in your garden, you take the appropriate actions to give them the best chance to grow big and strong, such as providing necessary water, light, fertilizer, etc. After that, you must sit back and allow them to grow in their own time. You can't pull the little baby sprouts up to make them grow faster – nor can you rush an intention. It will unfold in its own time and in its own perfect way, and you must trust that this will happen. Interfering won't help!

8. Present Moment Focus

Even though you are working on changing your future, it is important to keep your attention in the present moment. In other words, your intention is in the future and your attention is in the present. It is important to accept and appreciate your current life circumstances while expecting a better tomorrow. Developing this attitude of gratitude will help you connect with the field of infinite possibilities and increase the power of your intention.

Chapter Seven:
Set Your Mind on the Goal

> *"A goal without a plan is just a wish."*
> – Larry Elder
>
> *"What is not started today is never finished tomorrow."*
> – Johann Wolfgang von Goethe

Now you know the real, very powerful "secret" behind achieving goals that lead to personal and professional success – the power of intention. But how do you know what to "make it so"? Is there a better way to decide what goals to focus that immense power on, rather than wasting time on things you don't really need or want? Sure! You must first decide where it is you want to go before you declare your intention to the universe, and that's the focus of this chapter: creating meaningful goals.

Try this: go to the airport, and simply ask for a ticket. I doubt the clerk will be able to help you if you do not tell him where you want to go, or when you wish to depart. Besides which, nowadays they would probably look at with you great suspicion and treat you to a thorough frisking!

In life, if you want to get to a destination but you do not have a GPS system or even a good, old-fashioned map, you will never get there. In business, it's exactly the same. If you do not have a clear plan, you will never achieve the goals you set. The process starts by clearly defining meaningful goals that translate into specifically defined objectives. You must then create appropriate strategies and determine the tactics that will allow you to achieve those strategies.

Confused? That's okay! We're going to cover each of these concepts in greater detail.

Types of Goals

Not all goals revolve around a plan for your business. It's a good idea to create goals for each area of your life (family, relationships, career, finances, spiritual, etc.) because all are important pieces of your health, wealth and happiness. Goals don't get in the way of your creativity or freedom; they simply provide a destination.

These are the types of goals you may want to consider for yourself, all or some:

- **Career:** What level do you want to reach in your career, or what do you want to achieve? Perhaps you wish to start a new career.

- **Financial**: How much do you want to earn, by what stage of your life? How is this related to your career goals?

- **Education**: Is there any knowledge you want to acquire in particular areas of study? What information and skills will you need in order to achieve other goals?

- **Family**: Do you want to be a parent? If so, how are you going to be a good parent? How do you want your partner or members of your extended family to view you?

- **Personal Development**: Is any part of your mindset holding you back? Is there any personal behavior that upsets you? Do you have self-limiting beliefs that hinder your success? Commit to growing as a person, before you grow a business.

- **Physical**: Are there any athletic goals that you want to achieve, or do you want good health well into old age? What steps are you going to take to achieve this?

- **Pleasure**: How do you enjoy yourself? You should ensure that a part of your life is set aside just for your pleasure!

- **Spiritual**: This is the heart of it all. Are your spiritual goals aligned with all your other goals?

If you don't have personal, as well as professional goals, there will always be something lacking in your life. After all, you don't spend every waking hour in your business, do you (I sure hope not!)? If your life is not in balance, it doesn't matter what tools you have at your disposal, you will eventually fail and be miserable. There must be a healthy balance between professional goals, personal goals, relationship goals, and family goals so your life is well-rounded and not focused solely on a single area.

Most people think I'm crazy when I tell them I have goals for my family. "Why," they ask me, "Do you have goals for your family?" Because I love them! Why wouldn't I want them to be part of my plan for life success? At my house, my husband and I designate Friday evenings as party night with the kids. No matter who shows up on our doorstep Friday evening, they are invited to participate. Family party night is the plan we've already set in place for Friday and nothing is going to prevent the achievement of that goal. There are rare exceptions but that's what they are: rare. And just so no one forgets about our commitment to our time together, I write it down and post it on the bulletin board, so my husband and kids can check to see what's on the schedule. By writing it down I am reminded of my commitment – and so is my family.

As you brainstorm through the different goals you are setting for your own life, make sure that the goals you set are ones that you genuinely want to achieve, not ones that your parents, family, or employer think you should want. If you have a life or business partner, you should consider what he or she wants, however, make sure that you remain true to yourself, and don't compromise your standards. You will never be motivated to achieve goals that don't perfectly align with your moral compass, needs or desires.

Goal Achievement

How do you get from where you are now to where you are want to be? There are six steps involved:
1. Identify your goal.
2. Meditate on it daily.
3. Plan your success.
4. Write it down.
5. Hold yourself accountable.
6. Devise measurable tools to track progress.

Let's examine each of these steps in more detail.

1. Identify Your Goal

If you don't know what you are striving for, how will you achieve it? Once you know what you want, success happens so much quicker!

Remember, you can't buy a plane ticket for "anywhere".

You need to determine what you want as well as the price you are willing to pay for achieving that goal. Some goals are available only at a high price and they require maximum resources of time, effort, money and motivation. What are you willing to sacrifice for your goal? Are you willing to push past boundaries in ways you never thought possible? Without this initial commitment, you will not succeed.

Truly understanding your goal and why it's important is the very basis of every successful entrepreneur's plan. Without this crucial step, you will set yourself up for failure. The road to success is not always easy but if your "why" is big, then your "how" becomes nothing more than a minor consideration. If your "why" is small, than any little obstacles that come your way will seem like insurmountable barriers and you will find it difficult, if not impossible, to tear them down.

You will get more done faster if you are clear on your goals. When you have clarity, your actions sync with the desired end results, using the grand power of intention and your declaration to "Make it so!". If you have clarity, you will overcome procrastination and do the tasks necessary to achieve your goal in its entirety – and the perfect circumstances will come along at the perfect times.

2. Meditate on Your Goal Daily

When you meditate on your goal each and every day, your subconscious goes to work for you. All actions you do that day become focused toward arriving at your goal, whether you consciously realize it or not!

Getting to your goal is nothing more than consistently taking small steps forward. When you place your goal at the center of your mind in the morning, and understand that you have a big "why" for achieving that goal, you make the right choices every day that help you achieve the desired end result.

Have you ever heard the saying, "What you focus on expands"? Focus on great things and you will achieve great things; focus on negative things and your life will be negative. If you are trying to lose weight, be careful not to focus on the pounds because they will expand! Instead, focus on becoming healthy. The same is true for other types of goals, too. If you worry about employee turnover, you are likely to make the problem worse. Instead, set your mind on ways to keep the staff you currently have.

Consider the size of your goal. You've probably heard the allegory, "How do you eat an elephant?" and its answer, "One bite at a time." Big goals are discouraging. Focusing on small things makes it easier to achieve the bigger objective. If your goal is to lose weight, focus on switching out one fat-laden food for a healthy dish or choosing not to eat that very tempting candy bar. Those are small, easily doable things. The same is true if your goal is to make more money. Focus on the small things first, such as saving a few dollars a day by not buying that venti latte and putting the money into a cookie jar labeled "Business Fund". Those pennies and dollars add up! Goal achievement must start somewhere; just doing one small thing on a consistent basis keeps your actions moving in the right direction.

Don't forget about the immense power of intention. You actually become the person you desire to be by subconsciously working toward your goal. When you meditate on positive and empowering goals, your outer world resonates around the focus of your inner world. If you decide what you want (as you'll recall, always the first step in achieving a desired result), you move inherently towards your objective; you and the goal actually merge to become a unified force that achieves real results – you become the goal and the goal becomes you!

Getting your mind onboard with your goals means meditating on it each and every day.

3. Plan Your Success

We all know the importance of having a plan in place to attain the things we truly want, yet only three percent of us ever create a plan for success. Why not?

Goals are like the guideposts along your journey to success. The more you think about your goals, the more you will find them manifesting themselves.

This is an important concept in nearly anything we do in life. If your desire is to obtain a driver's license, you must plan for it rather than just walking into the Department of Motor Vehicles and asking for one. You might take a defensive driving course and read over your state's or province's rule book; perhaps you'll get some hands-on practice by getting behind the wheel of a vehicle and taking it for a spin.

Most people plan weddings or birthday parties, when to have children or how to save money to attend college. However, most people do not plan for success!

A plan is one of the key ingredients in achieving success but even creating it, how many people actually use the plan? This is the most important thing you can do! If you don't take half an hour to plan your life, how can you expect to find time for that massive success you are envisioning?

You know what happens when you don't plan or when you don't prepare a list of things to do: you get nothing worthwhile accomplished. How many people do you know who don't make a financial plan? They just live day to day and try to save as much as possible. Then the years pass and before they know it, they are no further ahead at retirement age than they were after graduating high school. They never have an understanding of why they are broke after years of earning money. People who budget get ahead financially because they have a monetary plan to follow.

Success works the same way. You must plan for it. You need to determine what you want and the price you are willing to pay to achieve that goal. You have to make plans to achieve your goal and follow that plan daily. It's a simple, yet critical concept.

Planning your goals promotes a positive mindset and unlocks the potential to achieve them. If you have no goals, you drift aimlessly wherever the river of life sweeps you. But with aspirations, you speed down a predetermined course that takes you on the quickest route from Point A to Point B.

4. Write Your Goals Down

Your memory will fail you. Trust me. We are all human and none of us has a perfect memory. In order to attain peak performance you must write down your goals and all the actions necessary to achieve them as a reminder of what you are trying to accomplish.

When you write a goal down, you have made a commitment to yourself. It's on paper so it stares you in the face every day until you achieve it.

Goals and actions written on paper will burn in your subconscious mind as you review your task list daily. By writing it down, you crystallize the objective and commit to the actions necessary to accomplish it. You have given your goals energy just by giving them ink! This also gives you a chance to go back and review the results of your actions at a later time and determine if they worked (see #6, "Develop Measurable Tools).

Those of us who have put our goals in writing will accomplish ten times more than those who don't. Quit complaining about the lack of hours in a day and focus on what needs to be done, via your plan.

You will be motivated by clear ambitions you put in writing. This helps you overcome procrastination because they will be staring you in the face each and every day as part of your success routine.

Goals lead to achievement because they incite action. The more you think about your goals, the more they become your inner desire, bringing your subconscious mind on board.

Always use present tense words to describe your goals. Write them down as though they are now a reality, e.g. "I earn $50,000 per month." Even though you haven't yet achieved that level of income, remember that you must think positively in order to make positive things happen.

5. Hold Yourself Accountable.

It's not enough to simply decide on a goal, write it down, and meditate on it daily; you need to do something about it!

If it was your business and you had an employee with a quarterly sales quota to make, you would probably put consequences in place for failure to achieve the minimum. What will you do if you do not achieve the goals you've set for yourself? While you don't need to punish yourself for not attaining a goal, you should certainly stick to an action plan and give yourself deadlines for each step so you don't wander off track.

6. Devise Measurable Tools to Track Progress

One way to hold yourself accountable for goal achievement is to devise measurable tools that show you exactly how much progress you've made.

Let's say I decide on the broad goal of "becoming happier" in the next year. How would I reach that goal? Can I measure that? I would first need to determine just what makes me happy.

How about if I want to make $100,000 over the next 12 months? That goal is measurable, and I can break it down into an amount of $8,333 that I would need to earn per month and even a more doable $1,923 per week. It's much easier to focus on the smaller increments that add up to the bigger goal.

You must have a tangible goal. Just saying, "I want to be wealthy" or "I want to be a better person" doesn't work. Those goals are too vague and there is no way to define either the steps to reach them or what you wish as the end result. How will you achieve a goal you can't measure or track?

There are no "right" or "wrong" goals. You might be seeking the career recognition you've been working so hard to realize or maybe you want to earn a lot of money by creating your own franchise. Perhaps your aim is to find the man or woman of your dreams, start a family, purchase your own home, buy the sports car you've always desired, or reach any number of other personal accomplishments. Is this success? For some of us, it might be. Perhaps you have a different definition of what success means to you. Whatever that definition might be, that is what you will base your goals on. They are only frivolous if they are based on what someone else wishes for you and not your own desires.

No doubt you are ready to sit down and create some real, measurable goals that will make your life better in any number of ways, personal or professional. The following exercise will help you set your mind on course to attain any type of success you desire.

EXERCISE 1: Nine Steps for Setting and Achieving Life-Changing Goals

Remember that nothing happens until you make a decision and then take action to move toward the goal you've set. Here are nine steps to complete, in order to set achievable, life-changing goals for personal or professional success.

1. Set Long Term or Lifetime Goals

Where do you want to be in one year? Three years? Five years? Beyond that? The first step in setting goals is to consider what you want to achieve in your lifetime (or at least by some significant and distant point in the future). Setting lifetime goals gives you an overall perspective that shapes all other aspects of your decision making and actions.

Write down long term goals for your career, profession, finances, health, relationship, spiritual and family. Go wild with this task. Imagine every possible thing you could ever want or need and write it down. This will be called, appropriately enough, your "wild list".

2. Take Inventory

How will you know where you want to go if you do not even know where you are today? Many people live a life of denial. They wear an outer mask of satisfaction presented to the world at large, while inside their minds resemble a jumbled mosaic of discontent, most likely because they are living someone else's dream. Then there are those who have a lot of tangible things, but still complain about their lack and refuse to give thanks for what they do have. Both these situations are negative – and quite common. What about you? Do you need to put your life in perspective before you consider the goals necessary to achieve what you truly desire?

In order to take inventory, ask yourself the following questions and think deeply about the answers before writing them on a piece of paper or typing them into a document you can refer to later:

- What are the things in existence right now that make me happy?
- What is the status of my physical, mental and spiritual health?
- What is my financial position as of today?
- How secure do I feel emotionally and financially?
- Do I have peace of mind, or do I suffer from discontent?

- What is the status of my relationship with family, spouse, coworkers and friends?
- What are the best things about my career? What is the best thing in my personal relationships? What is it that might be a problem in both?
- Am I living my life the way I want my children to live theirs?

Once you have answered these questions with a great deal of consideration, you will be more aware of your current circumstances. This current situation is the starting block, your Point A. From here you must map your path toward the goals that will make you wealthier, healthier and happier.

3. Find the Why for Everything on the List

So far you have made a list of all you want, without really thinking much about it. Now is the time to start seriously considering why you want each of these goals.

There are a number of things in this world we imagine we want but when it comes down to it, do we really want —or need — them?

This question is critical. Sometimes we desire something simply because it is what others expect us to, in which case we will probably never be motivated enough to take the necessary actions to achieve the goal. Other times there is something that we think we want, but after expending a lot of precious time and energy for the end result we find it wasn't really our heart's desire after all. You will find a large number of retired people who reminisce on their lives only to discover they never accomplished what they really wanted to – and suddenly it's too late. That is usually because they were too busy doing what they never really wished to or living the life of someone else's dreams.

Don't make the same mistake! There is still time to change the course of your life. To safeguard against this same situation, perform the following exercise.

Exercise 2: Determining What You Really Want

For every point you have written down on your wild list ask yourself, "Why do I want to be it? "Why do I want to do it?" or "Why do I want to have it?" Eliminate any point on your wild list for which you are unable to articulate a compelling one or two line answer.

For the remaining items, read through this entire exercise, then do it and write down your results.

1. Start by taking a moment to visualize your long term personal, professional, health, financial, family and spiritual goals. Close your eyes and imagine all those things that would make you happy.
2. Think of your desires and aspirations. Choose one goal in particular and focus on just that one.
3. See yourself in the next year, three years, five years, decade or more.
4. See yourself and this one big dream coming true. Don't be afraid to dream big. What are the circumstances surrounding it? With whom are you sharing the experience? Is there a celebration?
5. Now feel the emotions, really feel what it would be like to accomplish this goal. How do you feel knowing you have achieved your big dream?

6. What does accomplishing this goal mean to you? What will it do for you? Your spouse? Your family? Your career?
7. What freedom will it give you? What joy will it give you?
8. What is your why?
9. Take a moment and relish the thoughts, feelings and emotions of achieving this big goal.

When you are finished, open your eyes and write down that one goal and the big reason why you wish to achieve it.

Feel free to repeat this exercise as many times as necessary to experience each of your life goals in a deeper way.

Now ask yourself the following questions for each of the goals remaining on your wild list and write down the answers. This is another way of paring down your list into a more manageable inventory.

- Is it really my goal – or is it set by someone else?
- Is it fair to everyone concerned and morally correct?
- Will reaching this goal take me closer to or farther from my life's larger purpose?
- Can I commit myself emotionally to this goal?
- Can I visualize myself reaching this goal?

The answer to all the above questions must be a big yes! If you can't answer positively for any of the wild goals listed, simply strike it from the list. Before you lament the loss of any goals, let me assure you that a goal not yours, or one that will harm others, or one that does not move you closer to your larger purpose in life is not worth pursuing. It's simply not worth the time and trouble. If you do not commit yourself emotionally to the goal or if you cannot visualize yourself reaching it, chances are that you will never achieve it.

Exercise 3: Ready, Set Your Goals

Now it's time to actually make a decision on which goals you will focus. Go back to your pared down list of goals. For each one that is remaining, ensure that it adheres to the following rules for powerful, positive objectives:

Every Goal Needs to be Clearly Written as a Positive Statement.

Instead of "I will try not to procrastinate in starting my own business" try, "I will work one hour each week on writing a business plan to present to the bank so I can gain funding for my startup."

Set Performance Goals, Not Outcome Goals.

It's important to have as much control as possible over the goal. It can be quite disheartening to fail to achieve a personal goal for reasons beyond your control. The only thing you can really count is your own performance.

Goals Should be Precise and Timely.

For each goal, attach completion dates and even times. Allow enough time to accomplish it without being too far in the future. Include amounts (of time or money or effort) so you have something to measure. This way you will know exactly when you have achieved your goal and can celebrate your success.

Break Long Term Goals Into Short Term Actions.

Long term goals need to be broken down into short term actions so you believe they are achievable. Goal-setting is one of those things that seems like it should be very simple, but can often cause anguish and aggravation. The number one mistake that most people make when goal-setting is reaching too high right from the get-go. There is nothing wrong with reaching high – in fact I encourage it. However, what most people fail to consider is the process of growth and development that must take place between where they begin and where they'd like to end up.

You wouldn't expect an infant to set a goal to climb Mt. Everest, would you? The infant must first learn how to crawl, and then walk. He must grow into a man and strengthen his body. Finally, he must condition himself both physically and mentally to handle the harsh elements and weather he will encounter on his way to the top of the mountain.

Unfortunately, many people try to make a similar, large leap when they set goals. They want to transform themselves from a position of wanting and fear, to a position of power and success in a short period of time, and it's just not likely to happen that way. I know it's not impossible – but the odds are against you if you try to reach too high, too fast.

Every large goal can be broken down into smaller, more manageable goals. If your goal is to climb Mt. Everest, you will first need to gain some experience mountain climbing, get into great physical shape, and work on your stamina. You will need to set aside a block of time to travel to Nepal and perhaps hire some guides.

These are smaller goals but even those steps can be broken down further into buying books about mountain climbing, taking classes to educate yourself on hiking and rappelling, joining a gym to get in shape, starting a healthy eating plan, etc.

Successful goal-setting is as easy as learning how to identify the mini goals that compose each larger goal, and focusing your efforts on those first. Giving most of your attention to the smaller steps along the journey will result in less stress and much quicker progress. Keep your larger goal as your ultimate focus, however. This is your why, and the real motivator.

Go back to your list of goals and break each of them down into smaller, more achievable action steps.

Create Good, Better, and Best Goals.

Don't just set one goal for each area of your life you wish to change; set a minimum, a target and a mind blower sub-goal. Each large goal should include a subset of three goals for a good, better, and best outcome.

Remember that a positive mindset is the fundamental principle that makes pushing forward through any goal possible. You can't predict the obstacles and distractions that will block your path. Even with the best of intentions, you might not hit the monthly goal you set. Instead of being left with a down-and-out feeling that might cause you to give up on the larger goal entirely, having a subset list of three goals allows you to move on to the next. A "mind blower" goal would be the accomplishment of all the tasks on your list and if you achieve that, you can celebrate without feeling discouraged that the initial target goal was too low. Celebrating achievements is a positive reinforcement and a wonderful way to stay motivated on your way to ultimate goal.

Goals Must Include Action Steps.

A goal without action is useless. Without taking action, nothing will ever be accomplished.

You also need the right attitude while taking the necessary steps to achieve expected results. Your attitude is like a booster that propels you forward but keeps you on the straight and narrow. Action is the power to keep your journey going. A good attitude while you take the necessary steps forward provides the fuel necessary to stick with your goal and achieve success.

Celebrate Goal Achievements.

It's extremely important to celebrate when you achieve any goal, large or small. This builds self-confidence and motivation to keep you moving forward, on to the next goal, and then the next. Remember to take time to enjoy the satisfaction of achieving a goal because that provides positive reinforcement that will have you looking forward to setting and attaining the next one.

Chapter Eight:
Techniques for Resetting the Clock

> *"Time is what we want most, but what we use worst."* – William Penn

It's all well and good to have dreams and lofty aspirations for achieving monumental and powerful life-changing goals. But a common complaint that prevents many of us from ever getting started on them is a lack of time. How often do you find yourself running out of time? Weekly? Daily? Hourly? For many, it seems that there's just never enough time in the day to get everything done.

Time management is an essential skill that helps you keep your work under control, at the same time that it helps you keep stress to a minimum. Time management is life management.

No success is possible without time management or the means to organize the tasks necessary in your life. Have you ever met a successful business owner who was disorganized? Impossible. They would not succeed, at least not over the long term.

Your attitude toward time has enormous impact on your behavior and choices. Decide here and now to take control over the sequence of events in your life rather than be controlled by time. You are free to choose the task you accomplish next, so it's best to choose wisely, according to what is most important.

When you know how to manage your time, you gain control of your day. Rather than busily working here, there, and everywhere (and ultimately not getting much done along the way), effective time management helps you choose what to work on when. This is essential if you wish to achieve anything of real worth.

Just as the power of intention begins with a decision, so does time management. You are the one who decides how to spend your time, what you wish to do with it, and whether or not it's an efficient use of the hours in each day. You can decide to become an expert at time management, create an intention, and use your commitment and motivation to success to ensure it happens.

We would all love to have an extra couple of hours in every day. Since that is impossible, we need to work smarter on things that have the highest priority, and then create a schedule that reflects our work and personal priorities. With this in place, we can work in a focused and effective way, and really start achieving those goals, dreams and ambitions we care so much about.

The ultimate goal is to spend quality time at work and quantity time at home. The real purpose of time management, then, is to enable you to spend more time with the people you care about, doing the things you enjoy. The more time you spend with people you love, doing the things you love, the happier you will be.

You can find balance between home life and work, but you must make it a conscious effort. I vowed I would never trade time for money, yet when I opened my first chiropractic practice, I quickly became a slave to my business. My goal was to have both time and money, not one without the other. It took quite a while, but I finally learned to create a successful system, employ it, and then let it, with my employees as leaders, do the majority of heavy lifting while I focused on my number one priority: family.

The following tips and techniques represent how I learned to take control of my time and take back my life. I hope there's a few useful nuggets here you haven't heard before that will help you do the same.

1. Work Time is Work Time

Do you waste time at work? Perhaps you are not as productive as you could be in accomplishing your day-to-day goals. Chances are there is time left on the clock that you don't use to its full advantage.

Work all the time you are at work so you can do things you enjoy at home. Put your head down and accomplish what needs to be done, right away, every day. Start early, stay late, but don't waste time. Stop wasting time in idle chatter or daydreaming – this is time away from your family, necessary, but still hours of which your family is deprived.

Now, let's consider how often you are distracted at work. If you find yourself chuckling at the thought of the miniscule amount of time you aren't distracted, you are not alone. Most of us are distracted several times, if not dozens of times or more, every day. We get emergency emails and phone calls that add extra tasks to our to-do lists. We take breaks to browse the Internet, co-workers walk into our office for a quick chat, or send us amusing instant messages.

It doesn't matter where you work or what you do, you probably deal with distractions on a daily basis, even when your office is at home. These distractions are costly. Depending on the complexity of your work, regaining concentration after a distraction can take quite a while – if we can even manage to get back to the task at hand before it's time to quit for the day. If we're distracted ten times a day for ten minutes at a time, multiply those two amounts and you'll find an hour and forty minutes of wasted time. It's easy to see why we sometimes don't get much quality work done.

Learning how to minimize distractions can dramatically increase your productivity and effectiveness, as well as reduce your stress. Without distractions, you can get into the flow of your tasks, produce high-quality work, and achieve more than you ever thought possible.

Here are the most common distractions we face at work, and strategies for minimizing or eliminating them.

Email

While email is incredibly useful, it's also one of the biggest work distractions we face. Many of us could spend entire days simply reading and responding to electronic messages.

The solution? Schedule email time. Minimize this distraction by setting aside specific times to check and respond to email messages. For instance, you could check your inbox when you first arrive at work, at lunch, and right before you leave, and specify a half-hour slot every day to respond to your messages. If you do this, let co-workers and customers know they will need to contact via another method of communication if they need an urgent response.

Schedule your time for checking and responding to email at periods of low productivity. There are certain times of day when you probably do your best work or the phones don't ring quite so often. Some people work best in the morning, others are more productive late at night. Schedule email time during your least productive periods and save your peak hours for doing creative, high-value tasks.

Turn emails into actions. If an email message requires you to do something that will take more than a few minutes, add it as a new action to your to do list so it doesn't distract you each time you check your inbox.

Keep your email program closed when you're not using it – or at least turn off the visual or audible alerts that distract you. This eliminates the temptation to check it constantly and see what you're missing.

Most email programs will also allow you to fetch new email manually with a "send/receive" button, or will allow you to set it to get new email automatically at certain times of the day (every three hours, for example). Use these specifications to lose email distractions and add more productivity to your day.

Disorganization

A disorganized desk or office can be very distracting. When your work space or work life is cluttered and jumbled, your mind feels the same way. It is difficult to think and plan clearly in the midst of chaos. Getting organized is a topic that could easily fill books, and it does! If you need more help organizing your office, hire a professional or read more on the topic and then put those tips into action. The sooner you make a place for everything and put everything in its new home, the sooner you can bring your focus back to high priority tasks.

Instant Messaging

Instant messaging (IM) is a very powerful business tool if it's used in the right way, for the right reasons, but many times it's just a way for coworkers to interrupt you without having to get up and walk into your office.

If you use instant messaging as part of your work environment, get into the habit of only accessing it for short, quick queries. It's often better to use email or the phone for more complex ones.

Also, if you find yourself distracted by IM, consider setting specific times during the day when you will be available, just like email. When you don't want to be contacted, leave it off or set your status to busy or away. If people need to contact you, make sure they know your dedicated hours for IM.

Phone Calls

The ring of the phone has become almost like Pavlov's bell for some people – they think they must answer it, even if they are concentrating on something important.

Minimize phone call distractions by turning off your phone (not only your land line but your cell phone, too) during peak work hours. Or, let your team know that you won't take nonessential calls between specific times, such as from noon to two in the afternoon. If you have the luxury of an assistant who is in charge of answering phone, let her or him know when you wish to be interrupted and when you don't. Alternatively, those who answer the phone in your stead could use IM to ask if you can be interrupted or find a coworker available to take the call. If they are concentrating on a difficult task, they can easily take a ten minute reprieve without losing the thread of their work.

The Internet

Browsing the Web can take enormous chunks of time from anyone's day, and when we start looking on the Internet for one thing, it's easy to get lost for twenty minutes or more down a rabbit hole of interesting information.

The best solution? Close your Internet browser. Eliminate this distraction by keeping your browser window minimized or closed when you have no specific need to be online. If you repeatedly check personal email, or go on social networking sites like Facebook or Twitter, then log out of your account. If you're forced to take those few extra seconds to log in each time you wish to access them, it may remind you that you're not focusing on more important tasks.

However, bear in mind that tools like Twitter, Facebook and LinkedIn are increasingly useful for staying in touch with people and events in your industry. Just make sure that you only check these sites at set times of the day, for instance, before lunch and at the end of the day, just before you shut down your computer.

Distractions From Co-workers

Close your office door to keep people from casually stopping by for a chat. If they knock or come in anyway, explain that when your door is closed, you shouldn't be disturbed unless there's an emergency. A sign on your office door may also help – and a visible sign is a great way to keep family from interrupting you in a home office when you are concentrating on a challenging task.

One caveat: if you are a manager, there's clearly a tension between this and – very importantly – making sure that your door is always open to members of your team. Consider working from home or in a conference room when you don't want to be disturbed and post the time when you will be available.

Work Environment

Windows, a busy highway, or loud coworkers may all contribute to a distracting work environment. Sometimes you just need to shut the blinds, plug into a pair of earphones or turn on some soothing, nondescript background sounds. If you are able to, take your work outside and get it done in a quiet corner of your backyard or courtyard at your office building. This takes you out of the direct flow of traffic and could help you concentrate better.

Other Projects and Tasks

An overwhelming to do list looming over your head can represent a major distraction during the workday. This could cause you to procrastinate simply because you have so much to do, which further lowers your productivity.

Prioritize the list. Commit to accomplishing the two most important tasks on your list every day. For those things that are lower on the priority list or tasks that others can accomplish, delegate. Learning to delegate is important for managing an overwhelming list of tasks and projects; it also helps even the workload and use each team member's greatest strengths.

Tiredness

Coming to work well rested is vital to having a productive day and it's also important for your health.

The obvious solution to this distraction is getting enough sleep. Many people say they don't need more than a few hours each night but when you're tired, it's very easy to become distracted.

There were times when I was working as a school teacher and taking University classes, in addition to being a wife and mother, when there was simply not enough time to get it all done. Many nights I got a couple hours sleep at most – or no sleep at all. Rather than increasing my productivity, I found that this grueling schedule actually did the opposite – I was reading the same paragraphs over and over again because my tired mind just couldn't make sense out of the words. Sometimes it's best to put off a few tasks in order to catch up on sleep. You'll awake the next day refreshed and ready to tackle whatever needs to be accomplished.

Stay hydrated. When you don't drink enough water and become dehydrated, you may not think clearly. Dehydration can also make you feel physically tired and less alert. Keep a water bottle on your desk, and drink from it regularly during the day; fill it up several times and make sure you finish it all.

If you're tired in the middle of day (typically this occurs in the hour or so after lunch), go outside for a walk. Getting some fresh air and moving your body gives you a boost of energy while clearing your mind.

Watch your diet. What you put in your body often influences how you feel. For example, heavy, fat-laden lunches tend to make you tired; instead eat smaller, healthy snacks throughout the day and don't load up on fat and carbs during your lunchtime break.

2. The Psychology of Time Management

Your outer life is a mirror image of your inner life. So if one is scattered or disorganized, so is the other. But conversely, if your mind envisions you doing something, then you can most certainly accomplish it. This all goes back to the power of intention. If you want to see life differently, you need to change your inner life. Your inner life is how you see your outer life.

By now you know that you will never get anywhere if your car never leaves the garage. You must overcome procrastination and actually take a few steps down the path to success if you have any intention of achieving your goals.

The key to motivation can be found in its root word, "motive". To develop sufficient desire, you must be motivated by the benefits you will enjoy. You must want those benefits badly – and that's why it is so important to list the "why" for every goal you've set for yourself.

Of course, motivation is only effective if you make the time to use it! Motivation and action are both requirements for achieving goals.

Four Reasons for Practicing Effective Time Management

Do you really know how you spend each day? You might be surprised when you make a point of detailing each minute – or at least each hour.

Pick one day to keep track of how you spend your time. You might discover that you spend five hours managing interruptions and dealing with emergencies, and four hours doing actual work. This assessment shows you that you have only four productive hours each day to achieve your most important tasks. That's not a very big chunk out of a twenty-four day, is it?

Could effective time management give you an extra couple hours each and every day to work toward your major life goals? Sure! And look how managing your time (instead of allowing it to manage you) adds up over the long run:

1. Gain two extra hours each day.

This equates to 10 – 12 minutes per day for every minute of planning, so if you use 10 minutes to plan, 12 x 10 equals 120 minutes. Over one year, an extra two hours per day is like adding three months of productivity to your schedule!

2. Improve productivity and performance.

You will increase your productivity and efficiency by 25 percent or more and thus your income is likely to increase 25 percent, too!

3. Increase your sense of control.

You will have more energy and less stress by taking back control of your time – and your life. You will gain a sense of power and believe that you can accomplish anything. The more skilled you become at managing your time, the more positive you will be and that translates to greater success and happiness.

4. Have more time for your family.

More time in your day means more time for your family, doing things you enjoy with the people you love.

Become the master of your life just by gaining a couple extra hours per day!

Three Mental Barriers to Managing Time

Unfortunately, even though most of us realize the need to better manage our time, we fight it due to several silly reasons:

1. Worries about a lack of natural spontaneity.

This is a common excuse for someone who chooses not to discipline himself. The truth is, the better organized you are, the more apt you are to have the time and inclination to be spontaneous, feel relaxed, and enjoy your free time. You will also be more flexible and apt to deal better with change.

2. *Negative programming.*

Your parents may have labeled you as disorganized, perpetually late, or messy. As an adult you use the excuse of "that's just the way I am." No one is born neat, organized, or punctual. You may have developed bad habits, but habits can be changed. It takes twenty-one days to change a habit. Time management is a skill that we learn with practice and discipline.

3. *Self-limiting beliefs.*

Many people believe they don't have what it takes to be an effective time manager. That, however, is simply an excuse. There is no genetic component to time management, which is very much a product of your own control, motivation and desire.

How to Control Your Time

Remember Scarlett O'Hara in *Gone With the Wind*? She effectively summed up an important aspect of time management when she said, "After all, tomorrow is another day." Every day is a new beginning. We never know what things might happen that we didn't plan on and how much time they will take from the day's schedule. The following is a summary of the main areas of time management over which we have some degree of control, if only we *take* control of them.

Goal Setting

To manage time effectively, you need to set goals. When you know where you're going, you can then figure out what exactly needs to be done to get there and in what order. Without proper goal setting, you'll fritter your time away on a confusion of conflicting priorities.

People tend to neglect goal setting because it requires time and effort. What they fail to consider is that a little time and effort put in now saves an enormous amount of time, effort and frustration in the hours to come.

Prioritization

Face facts: you simply can't accomplish everything you want to get done in a single day. Prioritizing what needs to be done is especially important. Without this attention to detail, you may work very hard, but you won't achieve the results you want because what you are working on is not of strategic importance.

Most people have a to-do list of some sort. The problem is the list is just a collection of things that need to get done without a thought as to what's most important. There is no rhyme or reason to the list and, because of this, their work schedule is just as unstructured.

How do you work on to-do list tasks – top down, bottom up, easiest to hardest? To work efficiently you need to work on the most important, highest value tasks. This way you won't get caught scrambling to get something critical done as the deadline approaches. When I opened my first chiropractic clinic and rent was due, that made the task of getting clients through the door the highest priority! Sometimes it's pain that elevates one to-do, to a place of higher rank on the priority list.

Manage Interruptions

Having a plan and knowing how to prioritize it is one thing. The next issue is knowing what to do to minimize the interruptions you are sure to face during any given day. It is a widely recognized fact that managers enjoy very little uninterrupted time to work on high priority tasks. There are phone calls, information requests, questions from employees, and a whole host of other events and situations that crop up unexpectedly. Some do need to be dealt with immediately, but others are better managed through delegation or scheduling.

However, some jobs require that you are available when others need help, and interruptions are a natural and necessary part of professional (or even personal) life. Do what you can, sensibly, to minimize interruptions, but make sure you don't scare people away from communicating with you when they should.

Procrastination

"I'll get to it later" has led to the downfall of many a good entrepreneur. After too many "laters" the work piles up so high that even making a dent in the pile seems an impossible task.

Procrastination is as tempting as it is deadly. The best way to beat it is to recognize that you do, indeed, procrastinate. We all do. It's human nature. Then you need to figure out why. Perhaps you are afraid of failing. Some people are actually afraid of success and purposely never accomplish what they know they should, due to fear of failure.

Once you know why you procrastinate then you can plan to reverse that habit. Reward yourself for getting tasks done, and remind yourself regularly of the horrible consequences of leaving those boring tasks for later!

On the flip side, there are times when procrastination can save us from doing things of low value. Creative procrastination is the act of deciding on what you are *not* going to do now – if ever. This can help you reduce the amount of time you spend on useless things, like watching television. It can also serve to ensure that you are appointing the right person to the right job. If you are terrible with numbers, it might be best to pay an accountant to do your books and save yourself money later, when the tax man comes calling!

Scheduling

Much of time management comes down to effective scheduling. When you know your goals and priorities, you then need to create a schedule that keeps you on track, and protects you from the stress of not achieving your goals.

This means understanding the factors that affect the time you have available for work. You not only have to prioritize tasks, you have to leave room for interruptions, and contingency time for those unexpected events that otherwise wreak havoc with your schedule. By creating a robust schedule that reflects your priorities, as well as supports your personal goals, you end up with a winning combination, one that allows you to control your time and keep your life in balance.

Plan Every Day in Advance

When you wake up in the morning do you dread the day ahead due to an enormous workload coupled with time constraints? If the entire day stretching ahead of you presents a daunting hurdle, break it down into small increments filled with small activities and check each off as they are completed.

When you think, plan, and decide in advance, this becomes the most powerful tool in overcoming procrastination and facilitating productivity. Action without planning is the cause of every failure. Start with the end in mind, and work your way backward so you can clearly see where you are going, before you even get started.

Planning actually saves time. Every minute you spend planning saves ten minutes of execution. So using ten to fifteen minutes to plan saves you about two hours per day. The first 10 percent of planning and organizing your list saves 90 percent of the time it takes to get started.

You can increase your productivity by two hours each day if you just work from a list. If something unexpected comes up, simply add it to your existing list (which you may want to prepare the night before). If you don't complete all the tasks on your list, put those items back on tomorrow's to-do list. When you do this, your unconscious mind thinks about it at night so when you wake up in the morning, you are filled with new ideas on ways to complete the task.

Another bonus to planning your day in advance is you will be one step closer to achieving the goals you set out for yourself. Because everything you do consciously or unconsciously supports your goals through the power of intention, you will find achieving those goals happens much faster with a specific plan of action.

The 80-20 Rule

Chances are you have heard of the 80-20 rule in some form or another. This refers to the fact that 20 percent of your activities usually account for 80 percent of your results, or productivity, or goal achievement. As well, 20 percent of the tasks you tackle will account for 80 percent of the work necessary to accomplish those tasks. So if you have ten items on your to-do list, two of them will produce the greatest value (80 percent of the total value of your time).

Examine your to-do list and think about the 80-20 rule as you prioritize the items on it. Often one task is worth more than the sum of all the rest. This should be the highest priority item on your list, the one you tackle first, the one that gives you 80 percent of the desired result.

Make a list of the key activities and responsibilities that you wish to accomplish. Decide you will work on those areas that will make a difference in your life *first*.

Having a hard time prioritizing your to-do list? Ask yourself the potential consequence of doing or not doing each task. This is another great way to evaluate your list so you can determine which tasks belong in the top 20 percent.

Quit spending time on the more trivial stuff. I know it's tempting to get the little things out of the way (the bottom 80 percent) and present yourself with more checked-off items than to-dos, but procrastination on the really important stuff (the top 20 percent) isn't the way to effectively manage your time. We perceive this as self-gratifying when, in reality, it is self-destructive. Habits are hard to break. If you choose to start each day with low value tasks, you will develop that habit and it will be difficult to re-prioritize those tasks based on the system outlined here. The most valuable task you can do each day is the most complex, but the payoff is much larger. Refuse to work on any task prioritized in the bottom 80 percent of your list until the top 20 percent of the items are done.

When you start to work on a highly valuable task, you are sure to find that your motivation increases. Your mind naturally enjoys the challenge of working on something that makes a real difference in your bottom line. When you see results, you feel proud and satisfied. This, in turn, makes you more motivated to start your day focusing on high value tasks and, voila! A good habit is formed.

The ABCDE Prioritization Method

The more thought you put into planning your activities before you begin doing, the more important things you will do and the faster you will accomplish them. The ABCDE formula is based on the Franklin Covey method and represents a solid, very effective way to overcome procrastination.

The technique is simple. Write out a list of to-dos for the day and give each one a priority of A, B, C, D or E based on the following definitions of each:

A Tasks: These are very important tasks, our "must-do" items. If we don't accomplish these, there will be serious consequences. If you have more than one A task on your list, then further prioritize those items with numbers by marking them as A.1, A.2, etc. A tasks are things like satisfying a promise to a customer or completing a presentation scheduled for the same day.

B Tasks: These task are ones you should do but there are only mild consequences if they don't get done. Never focus on a B task if any of your A's are not yet completed. A "B task" might be something like following up with a customer who hasn't directly requested you give him a call.

C Tasks: These represent the tasks that would be nice to accomplish but there is no consequence at all if they don't get done. For example, lunch with a friend would be a C task because it has no effect on work life or goals.

D Tasks: These are things you can delegate to someone else, the things you don't have to personally accomplish. A simple task such as cleaning the break room or filing a stack of paperwork on your desk could be considered D tasks.

E Tasks: These tasks could be eliminated altogether without consequence. They may have been important at one time but are not anymore. E tasks are often those things you do purely out of habit. If you, as the CEO of a company, are personally shopping for office supplies like tissues or paper towels, this task needs to be eliminated from your list. Have your administrative staff do the shopping or set up an automatic monthly shipment. When you focus on E tasks, you are taking time away from doing something of actual value.

The key to using ABCDE for the effective management of time, is disciplining yourself to focus on A tasks and stay on them until complete. Don't allow yourself to be distracted by anything else until you can check those off your list. Your biggest job at the beginning of each day is determining that day's A1 task – and then completing it before doing anything else.

There are many methods for effectively managing your time at work. Try one or all of these and see which ones work best for you and the way you typically tackle your day.

The following exercise is also a great way to practice prioritizing tasks and then focusing on those that will produce the best results.

EXERCISE: Key Result Areas

Effective time management focuses on the tasks involved in Key Result Areas. When you learn how to do this, your success will skyrocket!

The following represents areas where positive results are necessary to succeed at a job.

If you do not succeed, you will underachieve and may even fail.

Key Result Areas of management:

- Planning
- Organizing
- Staffing
- Delegating
- Supervising
- Measuring
- Reporting

Key Result Areas of Sales:

- Prospecting
- Building rapport and trust
- Identify needs
- Presenting Persuasively
- Answering Objections

- Closing sales
- Getting Referrals

The starting point of high performance is to identify Key Results Areas in your work. They may vary based on specific job titles but you should be able to easily list the areas which are most important to your professional success.

After you have compiled your list, grade yourself on each area using a scale of one to ten, with ten being best. This shows the areas of your job where you are strong and those that require additional work. If you are exceptional in seven out of ten areas but poor in others, you will only be as effective as your weakest link. That means you must work on each area in order to truly be successful.

For instance, a manager who cannot delegate low priority tasks will often experience failure because delegation is a very important part of time management, and thus goal achievement. He or she will not be able to get the job done even if performance in all other areas is amazing.

No, none of us are perfect but don't defend your areas of weakness. Instead, identify them, state a goal and develop a plan for how you can improve in those areas. You may be one or two skills away from being the best performer, if only you can overcome the challenges you face. Fortunately, all business skills are learnable. Ask yourself, "What one skill could I develop that would have the greatest impact on my career?"

Your action plan for success:

- Identify Key Result Areas of your job.
- Write them down.
- Grade yourself from 1 to 10 on each one.
- Determine the three most important things you need to learn. Which

contributes to the greatest value of results you produce? Concentrate on them single-mindedly.

- Discuss your plan for successfully learning these three skills with a colleague or partner and obtain their input to ensure you are focusing on the right Key Result Areas.

Chapter Nine:
Your Script for Success

> *"It's all about the script."*
> – Jimmy Fallon

Would you perform in a play without rehearsing your lines beforehand? Probably not. After all, without a script, you are just winging it. If you had an important meeting or were scheduled to meet with an influential person like the President or Prime Minister, would you just go with the flow and say whatever came to mind? Of course not! You would prepare a powerful and impressive script beforehand.

If something is important, you always need to plan it. And that is why business scripts are so powerful; they allow you to prepare ahead of time for any type of encounter, but especially a sales presentation. Scripts are one of the most effective ways to transform anyone from an average entrepreneur to a superior, savvy business owner.

If you know the secrets to saying the right words at the right times, then becoming a master of persuasion is not too far from reality. And after all, isn't selling your idea, or product, or service to someone a method of persuading them to believe in your offerings?

Scripts are without a doubt the most powerful and profitable tool I have ever used in my chiropractic clinics. I believe developing well-planned scripts is one of the best ways to increase your bottom line. Yet most people are hesitant to add this powerful tool to their business arsenal. The truth is, whether you know it or not, you are already using scripts. And they could actually be hurting instead of helping your sales, if you don't ensure they are the best possible representation of you, your products, and your company. Ouch!

What is a Script?

If you deal with people on a daily basis, you are selling something, whether it's an actual product, service, or even yourself. So we will call all scripts for business "sales scripts" because that is what they are intended to do: sell. But what you are selling needn't always be an item of inventory; it can be nearly anything. You could be selling yourself to your boss when asking for a promotion, or selling a commission structure to network affiliates.

A sales script is simply an organized, documented system of selling your products or services. They serve to enhance the quality of your speech and thus your interaction with a customer. When you use a script, you will feel empowered to take control of the conversation and obtain the desired result – generating a sale.

Without a script, you are forced to think on the spot. I don't know about you, but I sometimes experience difficulty coming up with the exactly right thing to say at exactly the right time. Scripts help me deliver a message with consistency and achieve ultimate, reproducible results. This also helps me narrow down the elements which convert a prospect into a paying client and those that don't. Scripting is about how to improve the quality of your words so you use those that produce results.

An even bigger reason to use scripts is because you love the people you serve. You must know that your product or service will help solve a problem for your client or patient; by offering it to them you are enhancing their lives. Although you may know this in your heart, it might not come out that way when you are unprepared. If the words you use are poor quality, your prospect might not end up taking advantage of your offer, leaving you unable to enhance his life. If you are in business with a goal of helping others you can only achieve that by saying the right things at the right times in order to convince your prospect that he will truly enjoy a better life with the product or service you are offering. Scripts provide the right words when you need them most.

The number one reason that many businesspeople resist the idea of using a script is because they claim it feels unnatural or disingenuous. They have a negative mindset without even knowing what scripts are and how this powerful tool can help achieve their professional goals. The truth is, you can be motivated to sell and offer great products and services but if you don't have a script prepared, you are lacking a necessary ingredient in your recipe for success.

Let's back up a step before we continue to examine scripts and their development. You must first embrace the concepts of "selling" and "sales". When people think of sales, many of them give this word a negative connotation, envisioning the infamous used car salesman of old wearing a polyester leisure suit and a smarmy smile. However, if you are not proud of being a salesperson, you are erecting an invisible barrier between you and success.

You need to change your mindset and in order to do that, it's important to recognize the importance of the work you do in the field of sales. For now, I just want you to keep in mind that selling is a service to others. When you approach the art of sales with honesty, morals and compassion, you will be helping others; you lead and move them to an action that provides benefit. Be proud that you have something worthwhile to sell, which is not at all negative.

Now that you are willing to embrace the idea of pride in your sales ability, you must embrace scripting. And one way in particular to do so is by understanding the logic behind the principles. Powerful scripts work because human beings respond in predictable ways. The more you sell, the more you will see that your target demographic tends to respond uniformly to certain phrases.

The key is to find a script that works and then continue to use it at every appropriate opportunity. Read that sentence again because it is a $1,000,000 idea! There's no need to reinvent the wheel; a script that works can be used again and again to make more and more money. – and isn't that the real goal of any business?

In fact, you can create predictability with a sales presentation. That is what sales superstars do. They use the same sales scripts repeatedly because they are proven to work. Would you like to learn a script that generates high quality referrals over 95 percent of the time? I knew you would say yes. I knew this because I understand that people respond in predictable ways. Who wouldn't want a tool that ensures a 95 percent success rate?

Seven Ingredients of a Good Script

A script is really nothing more than a recipe. It's like baking a cake. You must first assemble all the necessary ingredients required for making a delicious confection. Every cake must include these core ingredients: flour, sugar, and leavening. The last thing you want to do is start making your cake only to find out a key ingredient is missing.

Just the same, you need to have all the ingredients on hand before you can create a winning sales script. Here are those seven ingredients:

1. Problem and Solution

What is the pain (problem) your clientele typically experience? How does your product or service solve this problem?

Prospects buy benefits and results. Your sales script must clearly show how your product or service makes life easier, more enjoyable, or just less stressful for the buyer. Focus on benefits, not features, because those speak directly to the ways you can minimize the prospect's pain.

2. Stories

Everyone loves a good story! It's the child in each of us. Who doesn't recall sitting in a classroom, a library, or in bed listening to a mesmerizing tale that swept us far away to a different place and time?

One of the most powerful sales scripts is one which starts with a powerful story. It can be one derived from your own personal experience, or simply the telling of someone else's story.

Stories help you connect to your client. They are engaging and powerful and, most of all, memorable. They can create rapport, suspend time, influence others on a subconscious level, bring benefits to life, reduce and/or eliminate objections, and even induce a trancelike state.

One of the most persuasive ways to communicate the end result of your product or service is to share a success story of someone in a similar situation as the prospect. Here is a great story lead-in for your script: "That reminds me of a client I recently worked with. He had the same concern you did…" or "Maybe you can relate to this. I was at home one night when…"

Having a hard time thinking of a story you can use in your sales script? Start a file, either digital or written, to record your stories. When one comes to mind, no matter where you are or what you are doing, take a minute or two and write down a little snippet that you can expand on later and add to your file.

3. Probing Questions

As you educate a client about your product or service and how it fills a particular need, it is very difficult to "tell" someone he or she really needs it. They need to come to that realization on their own terms, in their own time. People don't like to be told what to do. It is your job to guide them to the obvious conclusion.

The best way to do this is by leading with questions so that you take control of the conversation.

Use questions your client will answer positively. For example, if you said, "Mrs. X, wouldn't it be great if you could work less and make more?" you can bet that she will respond, "Yes." Follow this with another question, such as, "If you knew how to do that, you'd be rich right now, wouldn't you?" This allows Mrs. X to come to her own conclusion that what you are offering is in her best interests and she simply must buy it. We call this the "sum of small yeses that leads to the big yes to move ahead with a purchase."

Show your prospects what's good for them. You are the expert and you know how much better their lives can be when they buy your product or service. You are not misleading anyone, you are simply suggesting they need what you are selling to solve a problem and improve their lives.

Talk from a place of authenticity and ensure you are making the presentation because you wish for the greater good. It is your duty to relieve someone's pain. If you don't share an amazing solution to their problems, you are doing a disservice to humanity. It's not about you, it's about others. Find out what they want and give it to them. Remember, you are providing a necessary and important service.

Be prepared; make a laundry list of questions with positive answers and make them part of your script.

4. *Offers*

An offer isn't necessary in every sales script but if you are selling certain products or services, it can be a very compelling part of your presentation. An offer usually includes the components of: warranty, contract, payment terms, tuition, items included, and a call to action.

The key principle here? When there is money involved, always be completely honest and aboveboard. Your prospects don't want surprises when it comes to writing a check.

5. *Objections*

No matter the type of your business, you will always encounter objections during your presentation. It is not surprising to hear any client in any given sales situation, object to something, whether its cost, size, availability, or even based on personal vanity or pride.

If you have been selling your particular products or services for any length of time, you already know the objections you are likely to face. The great part of scripting is planning in advance how to handle them so you are not caught off guard, without a perfect response.

Start by creating a list of common objections. Here are four that salespeople in any type of business are likely to encounter:

- No money.
- No time.
- Need time to think about it.
- Need to discuss it with my spouse.

You must plan your script so you can easily overcome any of these objections. Plan in advance how you will address each one.

An advanced way to handle objections is to address them right upfront in your presentation, before the prospect even brings them up!

Professionals handle objections in their scripts even if they're not addressed because they know they will encounter them at some point during the presentation.

6. *Benefits*

If there's one thing really important to understand about selling, it's that people buy benefits, not features. Benefits sell – or educate – a prospect as to how a product or service can positively affect his life.

In order to make a sale, you must turn the features of your offering into benefits for the customer. For instance, you wouldn't tell someone he needs a television set because it has one thousand eighty lines of vertical resolution (in which case your prospect would probably say, "Huh?") but instead talk about how the display is really crisp and clear and he can easily see it from a distance.

Your product or service must deliver benefits to the buyer. These benefits might be tangible (things like making money or saving time) or intangible (providing peace of mind, energy, or confidence); provide results to an action ("What will happen if you take control of your pain? You'll be back to your job sooner."); detail the dire consequences of inaction ("What would happen if you died tomorrow without a life insurance policy?"); or be an advantage of the benefits themselves ("When you make more money you can pay off debt and then you can buy your dream home.").

7. *Calls to Action*

And finally, every good script must end with a call to action, what you want the other person to do. Of course you want the prospect to become a customer but it's not always as easy as asking for the sale outright.

Sometimes you can move a prospect to action by reversing the perceived risk. Sure, it's a risk to pay for anything but you can reverse that by offering a money-back return policy or guaranteeing a certain profit percentage after a set period of time.

It's a good idea to develop a test question to use at closing, too. This refers to a question that tests your prospective client emotionally, feeling him out about going ahead with the order. For instance, you might ask, "Do you want one or two of these today?" or "When can I book your appointment?" Always assume the sale is going forward but test the level of commitment before whipping out the sales contract.

Now that you know the seven key components of a good sales script, it's time to start outlining one you can use for your business.

Every sales script needs to consist of the following sections, in this order:

- Introduction
- Trust and rapport
- Identify customer needs
- Share benefits
- Close
- Objection handling
- Follow up

This list is not random. Understand there is a particular sequence to follow in every sales presentation. You don't want to put one ahead of the other in order to save time; stick with this outline as you work on developing your script further.

Communicating Your Message

How you communicate your sales message via your script is just as important as what's in it.

You will use persuasive techniques. Your body language, verbal and nonverbal communication, tone of voice, the words you use, strategic pauses, and eye contact all play an important role in the success of your sales presentation. You must connect with and influence each prospective client in a positive way.

There are nine elements of communication that are used in every effective script/presentation:

1. Introductory Sentence

How will you start your script? Try something like "Let me begin by thanking you" or "I hope we can consider this meeting a chance to get to know one another." Don't dive right into your sales pitch; take the time to set the other person at ease by making small talk first.

2. Manners of Speaking

What will your manner be as you start presenting your script? You have several choices:

talking, presenting, or conversing. Which you choose depends largely on the participation of the other person.

You could opt just to talk to your prospect, which is all about you talking at someone else. This is usually not very effective but could be your only choice if the other person refuses to participate. This is often a sign that he lacks social skills or isn't quite at ease yet.

You could present to your prospect, which is moderately more effective that talking, but very boring because there is no interaction; it's all about the product or service.

Or you could have a conversation. This creates energy and a paradigm shift to put you and your prospect on an equal plane. Conversations are alive and dynamic and the attention is on the other person and his needs, wants, desires. This is the ideal manner of presenting and the one toward which you should strive.

3. Power of Transmission

There are four ways in which humans communicate: words, tone of voice, pitch and pace.

Seven percent of how we communicate is done via the spoken word. Words can be abstract (difficult to understand) or they can be sensory (tangible). Focus more on using sensory words that speak to what someone can see, feel, hear, taste, or touch. For instance, in 1991 President Ronald Reagan said this about the national debt, "If you have a stack of one thousand bills four inches high you would be a millionaire. A trillionaire would have a stack sixty-seven miles high." Now that's a powerful sensory image!

Ninety-three percent of the information we communicate is done through tone of voice. This is why email is so ineffective as a communication tool; it is impossible to convey tone of voice via a written message. Tone of voice can soften a blow, indicate sarcasm, or add emphasis.

How do you speak? If the pitch of your voice is a monotone, it is very boring for the listener. Incorporating a variety of pitches (high, medium and low) keeps someone interested in listening. Pitch should fit the message you are conveying, however. Using a high tone of voice to talk about funeral arrangements isn't appropriate.

How fast or slow do you speak? If your speech is always the same pace, it quickly becomes boring. Vary your pace to add interest to our words. To relax the energy in the room, slow the pace of your words down. To increase the energy, increase the pace of your delivery. Warm and fuzzy emotions are best expressed slowly while humor is best delivered at a rapid-fire pace.

4. Punctuation

As you write down your script think about the punctuation you use to convey the meaning appropriate for each sentence. You can emphasize certain words or syllables. For instance, Winston Church, right after becoming Prime Minister of England in 1940, said "I have nothing to offer but blood, tears, sweat." Note how the commas force you to speak, with pauses in between each word in the list. If you wish to add punctuation to syllables, it might look like this: IN-CRE-DI-BLE. This reminds you where to put the right emphasis.

5. Power of the Pause

When you open up your presentation with silent spaces, great things often happen. Most people can't handle silence and feel compelled to fill every second. During a pause is when you can get them to make a commitment, tell you what they really want, or offer their objections.

Be sure you take this opportunity to breathe regularly (don't hold your breath while you wait for the space to be filled!), connect with your audience, and connect with the energy in the room.

6. Body Language

What is your prospect's body language telling you? The body never lies; it is the first to indicate feelings. In fact, body language comprises 55 percent of the communication between people so be mindful of:

    a. **Posture** – Stand tall and exude strength and confidence.

    b. **Center yourself** – Evenly distribute your weight between your feet and connect to your center of gravity. Don't become imbalanced by crossing your legs or leaning to one side.

    c. **Get grounded** – Ensure your legs are shoulder width apart with knees slightly bent. This signals you are ready, alert and present in the moment.

7. *Eye Contact*

This is the most important part of effective communication. They say that the eyes are the window to the soul, and this is so true! When you are presenting to a group of people, you can really ignite your audience simply by making eye contact, not with everyone but a select few, not only once but twice. This makes everyone in the audience feel personally involved. During an individual presentation, eye contact shows you are really present in the moment and is a very effective way of bringing the other person back to the present situation when attention begins to wander.

Conversely, if you avoid eye contact, people will think you are dishonest.

8. *Gestures*

Your body movements are visible to prospects during your presentation and that vision is very memorable. You can use body language to bring your spoken message to life. You can also transmit a lot more energy through gestures than speech.

When you want to anchor a specific point in your presentation, physically point to the ground, which emphasizes your words.

9. *Facial Expressions*

These are critical to the success of your presentation. Just as your body language is very visible, so are the expressions that cross your face. For a really excellent demonstration of how to use facial expressions to convey meaning, watch a silent movie.

When you master communication techniques that allow you to connect with a single prospect or a large audience in the manner intended, your presentation will be much more entertaining and powerful (in other words, successful at making the sale!). Remember that every little thing you say and do is on display; you may want to practice your script in the mirror before presenting to an audience of one or more.

Sales Script Techniques

There are 17 powerful ways to make a powerful impact with your sales script. These are techniques important to master in order to feel comfortable with using scripts and successfully close a transaction. These are the factors you need to focus on when devising a script that sells.

1. Credibility

Your prospect wants to learn about the benefits of your product or service and how it solves a problem. To present this information credibly, try telling a story. The stories in your script help you illustrate a common problem, present yourself as an authority on the subject, and offer a solution.

Your credibility helps the prospect feel comfortable enough to trust your response. To bolster your credibility, you might emphasize things like your academic credentials, professional experience, or achievements that addresses any issues your prospect might present. You can also use other people's credibility, if necessary, such as "Dr. Pane created this product after dealing with hundreds of patients who suffered from the same problem you have."

2. Emotions

You won't make a sale without first tapping into one or more emotions in your prospect. People buy based on the emotion they feel at the time of the sale. If emotions are strong enough, they will do anything to justify their purchase later, after those strong feelings have dissipated.

The most effective sales presentations tap into someone's pain, as we discussed earlier in the section about selling benefits. Present a way to relieve that pain, and you've got yourself a sale!

3. *Specificity*

Specifically highlighting certain benefits of your product or service can give you the edge you need to make a sale. You may encounter an objection such as, "My old car is just fine for getting me around town; I don't need a new one." Specificity allows you to successfully counter that objection with a statement that provides a solution to your prospect's problem, such as, "But this car gets three times the gas mileage, saving you lots of money at the pump."

4. *Build Massive Value*

Let the prospective client know how your product or service has been proven to relieve their pain or solve their problems. Highlight success stories of people just like them who are now feeling better, looking great, experiencing less stress, making more money, etc. The key is to present the value of your particular product or service as priceless because it can't be duplicated by similar items.

5. *Testimonials and Endorsements*

Testimonials or endorsements from someone famous or well known in your industry provide valuable social proof. This works better than you extolling all the virtues of your product or service. The prospect hears great things about your company and its product or service from a third party without a vested interest in the outcome of your presentation. When someone else endorses your offerings, you can achieve a level of influence you can't create on your own.

For presentation purposes, a picture of the person providing the endorsement, a magazine article, or a personalized endorsement letter, all provide powerful visual and social proof.

Testimonials and endorsements enhance the closing of a sale, too. Who doesn't want to hit the gym wearing the same clothes their favorite sports star does, or drive home in the same model car as an ultra-cool actor?

6. *Connect the Known to the Unknown*

An important part of the sales process is educating your prospect. One very effective way to do that is by connecting something he or she knows with something he or she doesn't know. This can be accomplished simply by changing the structure of your presentation.

For instance, let's say you are selling DVRs. You could remind your audience how difficult VCRs were to use when they first hit the market; many consumers didn't know how to record a program or didn't always have a blank tape available to record their favorite show. A VCR is a structure. It is a structure that allows you to record a television program. A DVR, on the other hand, is like a digital VCR. A DVR is a structure as well. Its purpose, just like the VCR, is to record a television program. The benefit of the DVR over a VCR is that you can record an entire series with the touch of a few buttons on your remote control, no **tape** required. Chances are when you owned a VCR you didn't record many programs. But with a DVR you are likely to record hundreds of times more shows. That's not because you have more motivation or discipline or willpower – it's because you changed the structure.

Think about how you can apply this concept in your sales presentation. What structures can you refer to as a way to illustrate positive change and close the sale?

7. Charts and Graphs

Charts and graphs are excellent visual tools that enhance nearly any sales presentation.

You don't have to use prepared, preprinted charts or graphs on glossy paper; sometimes drawing a simple image on a sheet of paper right in front of the prospect is very persuasive.

8. *Flattery*

Flattery is one of the most persuasive scripting techniques. Tell people how nice their smile is, how lovely their home is, how great their new haircut looks…all of these forms of flattery present great opportunities to build rapport. You must be sincere and truthful when giving someone a compliment, however, otherwise he or she will see right through you. This, of course, would do more harm than good to your chances of closing the sale.

9. *Preframe*

Preframing lets the prospect know in advance what is going to happen at the end of your presentation. Adding a hint to your script helps him be prepared later.

Here is an example of preframing in order to ask business referrals, "As you probably know I work with referrals. After you have received a great value from me I would like to ask you for others who would be interested in getting the same offer. Would that be okay?" Notice that you are not asking for referrals right away but merely preframing an upcoming request.

10. *Imagine is a Powerful Word*

The word "imagine" is a very powerful word. When you use it, you are giving the prospect permission to let her mind wander in the direction you lead it. Follow the word imagine with a description of a key benefit your product or service provides, in order to control the process.

As an example, you could say something like, "Imagine you are now sixty-five years old.

Because you got started today with your retirement plan you now have all the money you need to live the life you want. How would that feel? What are all the places you could go and things you could see if you just had the wealth necessary at retirement?"

11. Borrow Other's Scripts

I can't stress it enough! There's no need to reinvent the wheel – or the script.

Not all scripts work for all people, however. If your personality is passive and you attempt to use a script written by someone who has a dominant, in-your-face style, it is likely to feel uncomfortable and be ineffective.

12. Leading Language

The idea here is to create a gap in your script and let your prospect fill it in. Leave out a key phrase in one of your sentences so the prospect, himself, can step in and provide it. This produces a different level of influence when the prospect speaks personally about your product or service.

Try something like, "If you do what a millionaire does, you will get what a millionaire has. If you invest your money where millionaires currently have their money invested, you would become…?" The answer, of course, is "A millionaire." And that is the missing piece your prospect will happily provide. This creates a personal connection with the service you are offering.

13. Alternate Choice

Make your prospect feel as if he is in control by giving him two or more choices and where either option closes the sale. Once again, this creates a personal connection and really increases the odds that he will respond positively.

Try something like, "Would you prefer the blue one or the red one?" or "You can pay with Visa or MasterCard. Which card works best for you?" or "I have an opening on Thursday at four in the afternoon or Friday at nine in the morning. Which slot would you prefer?" In all of these instances, either option is positive and you enjoy closing the sale!

14. Appointment Setting

The purpose of using a script that sets an appointment is to…well…set an appointment, which is just one part of the sales process for many products and services. This creates the opportunity to either spend more time prospecting one-on-one, to order a custom fit product, or to make an assessment that will result in a later appointment. The focus is simply on setting the appointment, not trying to make a sale. This takes all of the pressure off your prospect, who is then likely to agree to a no-obligation commitment.

Ensure that the prospect realizes that keeping the appointment is valuable and presents a win-win situation for all involved. Understand that the benefits of setting an appointment are different than the benefits of the appointment itself, which will tout the features of your product or service. Some common benefits of an appointment are that it's free, it can be done in the home or office at a time convenient for the prospect, it provides a private question and answer session and it also allows time to truly identify the prospect's needs and wants.

15. Reverse Engineer

Reverse engineering is a process you can use when developing your overall script. Begin with the end in mind. From that place, backtrack and include each step that needs to be in the script in order to move a prospect forward to the desired action.

16. Practice Makes Perfect

Before using your script on a live prospect, you must first practice it. Practice makes perfect. Present your script word for word, time and time again until it feels comfortable and flows easily. When you are making a live presentation the last thing you want to worry about is remembering the words. The only things you should focus on during each live presentation are the subtle nuances that customize your script for each prospect. Professional actors don't need cue cards; professional salespeople should have their script memorized.

17. Visualize a Successful Presentation

The subconscious mind does not know the difference between a real or imaginary event. By visualizing a successful sales presentation prior to the actual event, you subtly influence the way you speak and act. Your script will successfully close the sale as long as you believe that will happen – and visualize it in your mind's eye beforehand.

Scripts for Success in Everything You Do

Depending on your type of work, there are several scripts you are bound to need in the course of a day or week or month. That might include scripts for:

- Appointment Setting
- Telephone Interactions
- Face to Face Time
- Referrals
- Objection Handling
- Front of Room (if you sell from stage)
- Conference Calls
- Recruiting
- Hiring

- Follow Ups
- Product Presentations
- Receptionist Phone Answering
- Money Collection
- Keeping in Touch
- Progress Reports
- Objections
- Customer Satisfaction Surveys

There is no such thing as having too many scripts. All are necessary, powerful tools to close the sale.

Before using scripts, I just couldn't figure out why sometimes people would listen to my advice as a chiropractor, and other times they wouldn't. It was frustrating because I was constantly wracking my brain trying to figure out why some people would understand the value of my services and why others wouldn't or couldn't.

When my patients did get it, I always got very excited because I knew I could really help these people! But I couldn't figure out what I had done differently in the two scenarios. I wasn't able to reproduce my success, the most important factor in developing a business that consistently operates in the black.

One day, purely by accident, I discovered it was all in my words (it wasn't until attending a seminar later that I found out this had a name: scripting). The difference between success and failure was using the right words. It was all about understanding that certain words should never be used while others were powerful every time. After that scripting seminar, I achieved even better results because I used my new knowledge to become a real pro at creating scripts.

I started to write scripts for every circumstance I might encounter in my practice and the results were incredible. When I created a script

I thought would work well, I honestly evaluated it, then repeated the words again and again, every time tweaking it slightly until it was perfect. Each time I used the perfected script I would get to a close. Some of the scripts I created were just really bad but by changing a word here and there, tweaking the order, adding pauses, changing my tone, etc., I found I could make them much more successful without scrapping the whole thing. What a difference this made!

Telephone Scripts

Everyone uses the phone to do business, and every call makes an impression on the person phoning, good or bad. Just one word, "Hello" can convey a ton of meaning. Talk about first impressions!

This is why telephone greetings are crucial. Prospective clients will come to a decision whether or not to do business with you in seconds of speaking with them on the phone. They will decide whether you are competent or inept, friendly or aloof, genuine or insincere.

Although many prospective clients dread listening to sales pitches via the telephone, you can overcome this with a simple approach that includes three key elements: pleasantry, conciseness, and sincerity.

If you answer the phone pleasantly, the caller is more likely to be pleasant in response. Many teachers of phone etiquette encourage you to change your physical self before picking up the phone; sit up straight and put a smile on your face because it will translate into a cheery phone personality. Remember that you are providing a valuable service to those you are calling; feel it so your voice conveys it.

You must make the introduction short. Nobody wants to listen to an excessively long greeting, and of course, even though a guide in the form of your script is available, you want to sound as natural as possible. I've called some professional offices where the poor receptionist was forced to say something like, "Good morning! I'm having a great day at XYZ Company and I hope you are, too. My name is Brenda and I'm happy to assist you with your needs today. How may I help you?" That's not concise and it certainly doesn't sound natural!

Many companies use telephone scripts because they find it useful for providing good service and better results. Some salespersons become tongue tied in the middle of a call and even forget to ask important questions. This is when a telephone script can come in handy. You don't want to get off the phone with a prospect and say to yourself afterward, "Dang! I forgot to ask about…" By using a telephone script, you can enjoy an engaging conversation with a prospective customer without worrying about what you need to bring up next. That's a great way to stay in the moment and really listen to the other person's concerns.

Using telephone scripts also helps you to keep the conversation focused. We've all experienced those calls where we get caught for long periods of time listening to a prospect who keeps on talking on and on about her family history and how she misses her children, and what happened to her when she was three years old. The best thing about scripts is that you will naturally incorporate techniques that allow you take back control of the conversation. Your prospect won't even think that you are not interested in her story because you've got a smooth transition to further the conversation right there in front of you, ready to use as needed.

In-Person Presentation Scripts

The script you write for an in-person presentation will be slightly different than one used on the telephone.

Part of any sales script should include a list of questions and corresponding answers. These questions allow you to elicit specific information from prospects without them realizing just how much information they are revealing. You need not worry about sounding like an automaton as long as you've taken the time to ensure your scripts are well-written, and that they promote a genuine, back-and-forth conversation with the prospect, which is of utmost importance.

Clients need to make the decision themselves, and that happens with them agreeing and saying "yes". When you are standing face-to-face with someone, lead your presentation with the questioning process so you get a number of minor "yes" answers first. This initial positive feedback is more likely to lead to a major positive decision in the end. Selling is really nothing more than a number of minor yeses that lead to the big decision when your prospect says "yes" at the point of sale. This is particularly important when you meet someone in person because it gets him involved in the conversation; you can easily and quickly create a back and forth banter that encourages deeper discussion.

Next, address your prospect's pain. What is the most common problem that your product or service solves? Let the prospect know you understand his pain and then provide a solution that uses your product or service to eliminate his problem.

Practice and repetition are the keys to successful presentation scripts. Learning the scripts you create, word for word, will make all the difference in your ability to sound natural and lead the conversation to a successful close. Learn them, feel them, and make them yours.

The Tie Down

This is a question at the end of a statement which demands a yes answer or isolates a specific objection. It must be inserted naturally into the conversation and become part of your speech habits. Examples of tie down questions include, "That was fun, wasn't it?" or "That feels better now, doesn't it?" or "Those look just great on you, don't they?" The actual tie down part of these questions are the phrases "wasn't it", "doesn't it", "don't they".

Inverted Tie Down

This simply refers to taking the tie down part of your question and moving it to the front of the query, "Wasn't that fun?" or "Doesn't that feel better now?" or "Don't those look great?"

Tie Down Tag-On

When your prospect makes a positive statement in the course of your presentation, capitalize on it by tying it down with a tag-on! For instance, if she says "These shoes do look good on me" you respond with, "Don't they?" You are tagging onto her question while affirming her positive comment.

Alternate Choice

Most questions have at least two possible answers (yes or no). Don't give your prospect a choice to answer negatively, instead ask a question in a way that confirms she is going ahead with the purchase: "Mrs. Jones, would you prefer one pair of shoes or two?"

The Porcupine

The way this question got its name will help the technique stick with you: if I threw a porcupine on your lap, you would undoubtedly throw it back!

The same technique is used in questioning. So, if Mrs. Jones asks, "What if I can't afford two pairs of shoes?" you would counter with, "Is money your concern?" Throw the question back in her lap and see what you get!

The Involvement

The idea here is to get your prospect to ask herself a question she would ask after owning your product or service, which is another way of asking her permission to go forward with the sale. Here's an example, "Mrs. Jones, will you be wearing this pair of support shoes at work or primarily at home?"

Adding these types of questions into any script helps you to move the sale forward in subtle ways.

Wouldn't it be wonderful to have all the necessary questions and tips all laid out before you before you begin your sales presentation? That's what you get with a script! You will be able to ask very specific questions and do so naturally because your mind isn't racing ahead to the next part of your pitch. All you have to do is memorize them and then start implementing them. Do this and watch your sales go through the roof!

I hope I have convinced you that scripting works because I have used it for years and it's made such a huge difference in my career. My income has grown astronomically by using effective scripts with repeatable, positive results. Before using strategic and organized scripts, I was making a healthy six-figure income. Once I learned that scripts involved a proven process and system and I began to use these simple strategies, my income grew from six figures to seven!

Now I just want you to imagine if you had sales scripts prepared for your business, what would this mean for your bottom line? What type of income could you generate if you never left another dollar on the table?

It's time for you to use the power of scripts to advance the profit potential of your business, and even allow you to delegate the sales process to an employee, freeing up your valuable time. Take a look at the following exercise to help you embody those traits that will make you a better speaker and presenter.

EXERCISE: Emulate Powerful People

To improve your portfolio you need to take "slices" of scripts from great leaders of the world and model your own delivery after their famous words, style and delivery – not the entire person, but the slivers that make that person's speech truly memorable and effective. Those slivers might portray compassion, confidence, bravery, self-assurance, fearlessness, etc. Whatever trait you want to convey, there is probably already an example of someone famous perfectly portraying it.

As you will recall, I mentioned that there's no reason we can't use other people's scripts as the basis of our own. When we emulate other successful people's scripts, their words, their actions, their expressions, their pauses, we inevitably become them in that moment!

You probably always wanted to grow up and be just like Donald Trump or Einstein or even Sam Walton. You wanted to be rich, successful, a leader. But this takes many, many years of trial and error. What if we could compress time to get from small to big very quickly? What if you could learn pieces of scripts from powerful leaders so that for a moment you became them, drawing from their strength?

Tony Robbins and Blair Singer did this all the time. They would take powerful "slices of scripts" from other people and use them to become confident, influential, idolized, funny – or whatever else they desired. They rehearsed other people's scripts until they knew the words, nuances, and gestures so well, they became someone else for a brief moment in time. And when they needed to recall that behavior, it was available, right on cue.

Remember, physical action is quite memorable. That's why you need to emulate all the gestures, facial expressions, pauses, and tones of voice that your role model uses.

There are three different states of presentation: physical, mental and emotional. If you change just one of those states in your presentation, you actually make a change to them all. Model the physical gestures of someone famous and if you do it perfectly, you will automatically model their mental and emotional states. That can be an incredibly powerful tool!

Studying influential and powerful people, in order to emulate their presentation style, has never been easier and that's what you need to do in this exercise.

For the following speeches, I encourage you to watch the video clip on YouTube (URL provided) and make notes about the physical and verbal delivery that you can imitate in your own scripts. Use these as examples of how to study speeches that exemplify the qualities you wish to embody during your own presentations.

Influential, Persuasive: Ronald Reagan

http://www.youtube.com/watch?v=YtYdjbpBk6A

> *"Today I say: As long as this gate is closed, as long as this scar of a wall is permitted to stand, it is not the German question alone that remains open, but the question of freedom for all mankind.*

In the nineteen fifties, Khrushchev predicted: 'We will bury you.'

But in the West today, we see a free world that has achieved a level of prosperity and wellbeing unprecedented in all human history. In the Communist world, we see failure.

There is one sign the Soviets can make that would be unmistakable, that would advance drama-dramatically the cause of freedom and peace.

General Secretary Gorbachev, if you seek peace, if you seek prosperity for the Soviet Union and Eastern Europe, if you seek liberalization: Come here to this gate.

Mr. Gorbachev, open this gate.
Mr. Gorbachev Mr. Gorbachev,
tear down this wall!"

Ronald Reagan was one of the United State's most beloved presidents. He was blessed with an uncanny ability to appeal to people of all ages and socioeconomic levels. His style of speech was easily understood by the masses yet extremely powerful in its message. Reagan was not nicknamed "The Great Communicator" for nothing!

This speech presented to the people of West Berlin contains one of the most memorable lines ever spoken, "Mr. Gorbachev, tear down this wall!" The Berlin Wall, built by Communists in August 1961 to enclose Germans within Communist-dominated East Berlin, represented the decades-old Cold War between the U.S. and Soviet Russia. Reagan's speech to commemorate the event represented the beginning of the end of the Cold War and Communism in Russia – a huge achievement for the then-president and former actor.

Although the speech was written for Reagan, he could never have delivered it so powerfully if he hadn't deeply believed in the words.

What made Regan such an influential speaker? A large part of his reputation as "The Great Communicator" was based on the dichotomies of his speech:

- A confident, but conversational, tone.
- Thoughtful, yet purposeful.
- Poetic, yet stark rhetoric.

Inspirational: Rocky

www.youtube.com/watch?v=uyTAfX7cniI

Rocky Balboa: *"Let me tell you something you already know. The world ain't all sunshine and rainbows. It's a very mean and nasty place and I don't care how tough you are it will beat you to your knees and keep you there permanently if you let it. You, me, or nobody is gonna hit as hard as life. But it ain't about how hard you hit; it's about how hard you can get hit, and keep moving forward. How much you can take, and keep moving forward. That's how winning is done. Now, if you know what you're worth, then go out and get what you're worth. But you gotta be willing to take the hits, and not pointing fingers saying you ain't where you are because of him, or her, or anybody. Cowards do that and that ain't you. You're better than that!*

I am always gonna love you no matter what, no matter what happens. You're my son and you're my blood. You're the best thing in my life... But until you start believing in yourself, you ain't gonna have a life..."

In Sylvester Stallone's 1976 movie, *Rocky*, he delivers a powerful message to his son that inspired millions of people in this tale of the good-natured debt collector and club fighter turned heavyweight champion contender. This is a classic underdog story featuring a character whose heart and determination made those who watched it believe him and believe in themselves. This movie is about how courage, determination and a willingness to do whatever it takes allows anyone to go the distance.

In life, sometimes this is the attitude we need to adopt. We all will be faced with challenges. Many give up on their dreams and goals because it's easier to blame others for their failures or lack of accomplishments.

As individuals, we need to believe that we ourselves have the power to do anything to which we set our minds. The road to getting there is not always easy but we must consider adversity as an opportunity to fight through whatever challenges with which we are faced. Why? As you get beat in the rink, and you stand up and start over again, something happens inside your mind. You become stronger and more confident that you can achieve all things.

This message is powerful and I encourage you to become Rocky in the moment when you doubt you can achieve greatness.

Studying "slices" of characters and famous people allows you to "impersonate" them, not physically but emotionally, in the moment of your presentation. Emulating them allows you to embody the same characteristics they are portraying, whether it's being fearless, courageous, funny, etc.

Sometimes when delivering a script, you need to adopt these demeanors in order to give your words more meaning and credibility and elicit emotion in your audience. Try finding your own example of a speech from someone who embodies the characteristics necessary for you to deliver a convincing script and do your best to make modeling that "slice" second nature. Think of it as rehearsing for an ongoing role!

Chapter Ten:
The Art of Selling and Closing

> *"No one limits your growth but you. If you want to earn more, learn more. That means you'll work harder for a while; that means you'll work longer for a while. But you'll be paid for your extra effort with enhanced earnings down the road."*
> – Tom Hopkins

Do you believe that selling is something that comes naturally to some people? It may, but that doesn't mean you can't learn the art of selling and closing every – or almost every – prospect with whom you meet. In fact, it may be simpler than you think. Just like anything you set your mind to, selling is a part of entrepreneurship that you can master. If you dread the prospect of contacting prospects, it's especially important to make this task a process so you don't have to wing it.

There are five steps that everyone uses in order to learn something new. They apply to learning the art of selling as much as they apply to learning anything else. These steps are impact, repetition, utilization, internalization, and reinforcement. They represent the elements essential for teaching yourself how to do anything, from learning a new language to learning how to sell and close the deal. Let's take a closer look.

Step 1: Impact

When you interact with someone, you are impacting them in some way. They are either watching you or listening to you, and that's a conscious effort at communication. However, what you say is likely to go in one ear and right out the other. You know why? It takes Step 2 to make something stick in the other person's consciousness.

Step 2: Repetition

Repeating something over and over again is the mother of all retention methods when you are trying to learn something new. If you say the same words or practice an action enough times, it becomes part of you.

The goal of repetition is to help you find the right words that work with your personality and presentation style. Certain words are very powerful and effective but you must put them together into phrases that are truly yours.

It all starts with repetition. Once you put a specific idea into words and ingrain them in your psyche, it doesn't take much to make them part of you. Say the phrases out loud, over and over again, each time paying close attention to what feels and sounds natural for you.

Step 3: Utilization

What have you used in the past to make a sale? Think back on past presentations and review the parts that worked. Utilize the same material you know is effective each and every time you make a presentation, and you can double, triple, or even quadruple your sales. Use it over and over again because it works.

Here is another benefit of using what you already know works. When you utilize the same material on a regular basis, it starts to become a part of you, without conscious thought. That allows you to focus on the subtle nuances necessary for specific client interactions, such as your tone of voice, pitch, delivery, etc.

Step 4: Internalization

What impact do you want to make on every prospect with whom you meet? How can you use that impact to move toward a sale? Think carefully about how you can utilize your unique technique to create a lasting impression when meeting with someone in person.

As long as you internalize your technique, it literally becomes part of you! You've probably heard someone say that an acquaintance sounds just like you. He or she is not you, but uses the words you do, those unique phrases and that delivery style which is associated with your persona. This is a good thing because it makes you stand out in someone's mind. Your impact should be memorable enough that every time someone thinks about the product or service you offer, a vision of you comes to mind.

Step 5: Reinforcement

You can never stop practicing your presentation. Some people reading this book will stop doing what works once they get to where they want to be. They quit practicing those techniques and tasks that brought them to a higher level. Once their income doubles, they stop as if they are done. "That was great! Now what?"

Professionals go back to the basics each and every year (or more often) to remind them of what works and fine tune the details. Think of your favorite pro sports team. Do the players use preseason training to sharpen their skills before the first game? Do they need constant and consistent training in order to play better? Do they need to sweat in the process? You bet they do! In fact, the more they wish to improve their game, the more they practice. And so should you.

Make yourself do what you want to do. Don't decide to be average and simply settle for that. A brain surgeon doesn't wake up one morning and decide to perform brain surgery. He dedicates years to learning the necessary skills and practices prior to doing the real thing (at least you'd certainly hope so!). Is he qualified to operate on your brain after sixty days of practice? I doubt it! It takes time, and the learning never stops because unique situations arise all the time. You earn an income in direct proportion to your skill. The surgeon uses a scalpel, a fighter his fists, a tennis player a racquet, a salesperson his mouth!

Your job is to learn what to say, how to say it and when to say it. You need to learn the steps and strategies to walk out of every appointment with the sale every time. Once you've got that done, you can reproduce your results and never again wonder *if* you'll make the sale.

The Secret Sauce of Sales Success

To be successful, every salesperson needs to develop or improve certain personal characteristics: appearance, pride, confidence, warmth, and self-assurance. These are the five ingredients in your "secret sauce" for sales success that really aren't so secret. Actually, it is quite amazing how simple these qualities are to improve, yet many salespeople who struggle don't take these "little" things into account.

How about your appearance? This is not necessarily about the clothes you wear (although you should pay attention to your dress), but the way you present yourself.

A first impression is everything, it will either draw people to you or away from you. Ideally, people look at you when you walk into a room because of your confidence.

How you present yourself is another aspect of appearance. Your voice should not be too soft and definitely not too loud. Always make eye contact when introducing yourself, and offer a firm handshake. Say the other person's name a number of times to yourself not only so you remember it later on demand, but to show him or her that you care enough to remember it. If you display warmth and compassion, you will hook others from the start.

Think about instances when you met other people for the first time. Some of them probably repulsed you from the very moment they opened their mouths or even from the first glance. Others may have made you feel totally amazed and honored to be in their presence. Which one are you?

You should be proud not only of how you look but of what you do. The profession of selling is time-honored and valuable. You provide a service that helps many people; be proud of it!

That confidence you exude when you walk into the room shouldn't evaporate the minute you start speaking. People must be moved by your belief in yourself and what you have to offer. If this is a problem for you, practice being confident each and every day. The more you practice, the more your confidence will come from a place of authenticity.

Your mannerisms need to be warm and loving. If you say and do everything in your job as a demonstration of your love for someone else, you can never go wrong. It's not about being pushy, which never works; this may produce results in the short run but in the long run you will lose more customers than you gain. Your sales technique should be strong, but always delivered with genuine warmth.

Could you be more self-assured? More than confidence, self-assurance comes from knowing that you are the best person you can be; in your sales presentation you must let others know you wish the same for them and their loved ones. Assure prospects that you can help them and offer them the assurance you provide through your product or service.

Nine Selling Stressors

Selling is often a difficult task; it can be considered a stress trigger in and of itself particularly if you are not comfortable with the process. The best way to deal with the stressors involved in selling is to be aware of them beforehand, and develop coping strategies that turn the negatives into positives. These are the top nine ways you might be unconsciously sabotaging your sales presentation.

Guilt

If ever there was a wasted emotion in regard to sales, it's guilt. Why would you feel guilty for selling someone a product or service that provides a benefit? The only reason for feeling guilty would be if you somehow trick a person into using their last few dollars to buy something they really don't need – and there's no way you would do that! You are performing a valuable service by offering others things that will positively change their lives. Be proud, not guilty.

Lack of Discipline

Discipline is the fountain of greatness. All good things come as a result of self control and personal restraint. If you want something bad enough, you will reach deep down inside and find the discipline necessary to achieve your goals. Remember that you have already come up with a really compelling reason why you want to achieve a particular goal; always bear that in mind as you do what is necessary to complete the sale and keep your business profitable.

Rejection

We've all got a fear of rejection; it's human nature. The reason we fear it is because we have experienced it at some point in the past. And I can assure you that you will experience it again! Not everyone is going to love your products or services and that's okay. Just don't take it personally. It's not all about you.

Disappointment

It's easy to imagine why you might get disappointed at the end of a sales presentation; after all, you just spent a lot of time with someone to educate them on the benefits of your product or service but they decided not to buy! Release your anger, your disappointment, your frustration; it certainly doesn't further your goals to let it take over your day or week or month.

Rather than show your disappointment, congratulate your prospect on their decision. Then use this opportunity to play on his emotional obligation. Hand him three of your business cards and ask him to pass them out to others who might be interested in what you have to offer.

Fear

We've already touched on this in regards to goal setting so you may recall that fear is the one, big emotion that keeps people from attaining what they really want in life.

In order to overcome this debilitating emotion, you must do what you fear most. Make a decision to do something that causes your gut to clench because, after all, what's the worst thing that could happen? By overcoming your fears, you become stronger and more successful.

Scheduling

You must make a commitment to yourself to use your time wisely. At the beginning of each day, write down the things you are going to accomplish. Remember that you need to give each task a priority level so you don't get overwhelmed trying to accomplish more than you can do in one day. Do what you hate – those things you will do anything to avoid – first thing each morning and then watch the rest of your day unfold into a pleasant experience.

Procrastination

Why do today what you can put off until tomorrow? That's a common mantra in today's society. It means that you are living yesterday, avoiding today and ruining tomorrow. Is that what success looks like?

If you truly want success, you need to start *today*. Allow yourself to only pre-plan one day of procrastination before you take action. That is the only time it's allowed – your one day of pre-planned procrastination in order to prepare for the actual doing. But even better, live by three words: Do it now. It takes twenty-one days to change a habit. Today is Day One…what new habit will you start today?

Peer Attacks

Is someone else jealous of you? Do they let you know it by their words and actions? Bear in mind that no one is jealous of a loser so you must be doing something right. Rather than buying into someone else's negativity, say to yourself (right now, please!), "I will never, ever again take advice from anyone more confused than I am." That goes for friends, associates, and even close family members. You know what you're doing; stay the course.

Appointment Cancellations

It's always disappointing when you make the time to meet with someone only to get that dreaded last minute phone call telling you plans have changed. Try to avoid this before it occurs. When you confirm an appointment, don't say, "I am just confirming our appointment for Tuesday at two PM." Instead, try, "Hello Bill. We have an appointment today at two PM and I'm excited to see you!" If Bill tries to back out, counter with, "Oh no! That time has been set aside just for you. I am sure you will feel better after our appointment. I'll see you at two!"

The Art of Selling

When you learn to be successful at sales, you reap a multitude of benefits. You become financially independent – able to do what you want, when you not, instead of what you feel you have to.

Just remember that making money is easy; keeping it is the difficult part!

Financial success also provides emotional stability. You will find yourself feeling happier more often and better able to cope with crises and the fear of the unknown. For most people, business success translates into spiritual fulfillment, as well. It can truly open your spirit up to receiving direction from whatever higher power you believe in and thus enhancing your life in ways you never previously thought possible.

So what does it take to be really good at selling? To be successful, every salesperson needs several key elements. They are:

- Prospects (Leads)
- First contact
- Qualifying process
- Presentation
- Handle objections
- Close the sale
- Upsell and Downsell
- Set the intention
- Referrals

Prospects/Leads

Activity means productivity. And in order to remain active, you need to work leads. Don't sit around and wait for leads to come to you. If your only referrals are coming from others, you aren't doing squat for your business (it is *your* business, right?). That makes you dependent on others and not in control of your own destiny. Take control of your own success; go out and find new prospects. These days there are a number of ways to do this, both online and offline; work them!

If you have a new product coming out, call everyone who has the old version of this product and invite them to check out the new stuff. People tend to want the latest and greatest and they will often upgrade with proper education on how this new product or service might help them.

A successful entrepreneur looks for areas to generate business, whether that's standing in an elevator, dining out at a restaurant, watching a sports game, or attending a social function, such as a wedding or birthday party. Are you looking for and using every available opportunity?

A great source of leads for nearly any type of business is real estate agents. Get to know one or more successful realtors in your area. When people move to a new area, they need to relocate most of their services. Why wouldn't you be the one to help them with whatever they need?

Associate yourself with like-minded people. Have you noticed that your co-workers and business associates have a drive similar to yours? There is a reason for this: like-minded people have an energy that, when multiplied, creates a fantastic drive to succeed. You will be naturally drawn to others who strive to attain the same goals you have.

First Contact

First impressions are made within the first 10 seconds of meeting someone. What impression are you making? You may want to practice your introduction in front of the mirror so you see what others see, and can correct anything that might be regarded as off-putting. Remember to repeat the other person's name several times with the first few minutes in order to remember it, then use it liberally.

Qualification

There's no point wasting your time prospecting people who truly do not need your service or product. It's important to establish the prospect's need right away – and make sure that you don't confuse their needs with your wants. Use this "NEADS" formula to qualify someone with a few simple questions:

- **N – Now**: "What do they have or do now?"
- **E – Enjoy**: "What do they enjoy doing?"
- **A – Alter**: "What do they want to improve or change?"
- **D – Decision maker**: "Can they make the decision to buy?"
- **S – Solutions**: "What is the problem I can solve for them?"

Presentation

A successful sales presentation is all about knowing when, where, and how to show your product or service – and this is also key for closing the sale. Don't get impatient or wait too long; anticipate the exactly right moments to present the right parts of your presentation.

Make sure your presentation is interactive. Selling is a participatory and involved process. We have five senses and it's best to get as many of them involved in the sales process as possible. Let your prospect see the product, try it out, hear about the benefits and actually touch it.

Handle Objections

There is no reason for you to lose a sale to objections (which we will cover in more depth in the next chapter). The successful salesperson identifies all possible objections beforehand and devises a response for each, being prepared to overcome them.

Close the Sale

Your goal? Get your prospect to see the benefit of what you are offering and then obtain a commitment to purchase. Until that point, you haven't gotten to the close, and you haven't done your job.

Upsell and Downsell

Upsells and downsells present an amazing way to take full advantage of a sale. Very few, if any, companies offer a single product or level of service. You can use everything in your inventory to make a sale, whether it's for a bit less or a bit more than you originally anticipated.

When your prospect presents a cost objection to the sale, present a less expensive option (downsell). In this way you may get a sale at a lower price point than expected, but you will walk away from your meeting with a sale nonetheless – and that's the goal.

Here's an example of a nifty upsell. Let's say you own a boutique and you have a customer trying on a pair of jeans. She realizes how amazing she looks in them. You then whip out the matching jacket and have her try it on. She falls in love with the complete outfit and you continue to build on this by dashing over to the accessories department and bringing back a belt and purse that match both pieces. Your customer threads the belt through the loops of the jeans and clutches the purse while turning this way and that, admiring her reflection in the mirror. Your job is to continue to upsell your customer until she finally says, "No, that's enough." This is a great way to increase the average dollar amount of your sales.

Set the Intention

Remember the power of intention from Chapter Six? You simply need to decide that you will make a sale today with a client who is sure to benefit from your product or service. The necessary words will come to you without conscious thought . Set the intention before you step foot into the meeting and witness the power of the universe aligning with your decision.

Referrals

But...after you close the sale your job still isn't done. Don't leave the meeting without asking for referrals so you can repopulate your list of prospects.

Don't just ask your customer in an offhanded manner if she will refer you to others; get specific! Ask her to focus on a particular group who fits your target market. If you are a better than average salesperson (and that's the point of this chapter!) your new customer will be more than happy to continue the relationship by providing you with leads. Don't let this opportunity be lost.

The power of referrals can't be overstated. All business success is a product of ratios. The more leads you have, the better your odds of selling more. Think about this: if you can close one out of ten prospects, that's a 10 percent conversion rate. If you can increase your conversion rate, (which you should certainly be able to do after reading this book) by only another 10 percent, you've doubled the amount of new customers your business will enjoy! And after you've closed that last customer, ask for two more leads.

Referrals are prequalified prospects. Doesn't it make sense to spend more time working prequalified leads than it does to cold call a random list of numbers?

In order to get the maximum number of referrals, you need to ask your current clientele the right questions. When you ask a question such as, "Do you know anyone who could benefit from our chiropractic services?" you are bound to get a negative answer. That's because your question was too vague – you asked your customer to consider the entire world! Instead, request that your customer focus on a particular group. Be specific. Try, "John, is there anyone on your hockey team suffering from a similar injury? If you would like to see them enjoy the same great results you did, please pass along my business card." This is much more likely to result in a positive response because your client is now only thinking about thirteen to sixteen people, not the entire universe! Ask your customers about where they work, what their hobbies are, or which sports they play. Do it with warmth and genuine interest, but use the information to ask for referrals from a focused group.

By the way, you can do the same thing with a three by five inch postcard. Add return postage paid, a short set of qualifying questions, and spaces for your clients to write in appropriate names, addresses, phone numbers.

The best time to ask for a referral? When your customer is happy: "Jennifer, I am so happy that you are satisfied with your new internet service and excited that we are able to save you money on your monthly bills. Is there someone else in the neighborhood who might desire the same savings?"

At this point Jennifer is happy, your company name is fresh in her mind, and she will feel good about producing a referral. Slam dunk!

Here are a handful of best practices to use when asking for referrals:

1. Send a thank you note. Better yet, send a lottery ticket – people remember sensational tokens of appreciation.
2. Handle any problems that occur immediately.
3. Call people back immediately.
4. Keep all promises you make (so don't make promises you can't keep).
5. Stay in touch with new prospects. Send them short messages via email, a newsletter, a card in the mail.

If you can get five leads from each of your current customers, you will write your own ticket to great success.

Telephone Selling Techniques

There are times when you need to make your sales presentation over the phone, perfect for those times when you simply can't meet with someone face-to-face or when you are trying to reach a business owner, but only getting through to a receptionist answering the phones. This is becoming more and more common due to a proliferation of Internet-only business models these days.

It is just as important to convert a prospect over the phone as it is in person. If someone calls and asks about your product or service – how wonderful! This is a great lead!

How you handle the phones is crucial to your sales success. This five-step process ensures you take advantage of each phone call.

Step 1: Answer the Phone

I recommend that your phone get answered on the third ring – not before and not after. If you answer on the first ring, the caller will be taken aback and may imagine you are sitting around with nothing else to do. If you answer on the tenth ring, it shows that you don't care. The third ring answer is proven to be most effective. Make sure you share this information with anyone else in your organization who answers incoming phone calls.

Step 2: Control Your Voice

Your voice creates a visual image for the person on the other end of the line. If your tone signals excitement and enthusiasm, that's the impression your caller will get. On the other hand, if you sound like death warmed over you are unlikely to gain a new client. Before you answer, stop. Clear your mind. Inject enthusiasm into your voice. Come across as happy and anxious to help.

Step 3: Acknowledge

Ask what each caller needs and acknowledge that right away by repeating it. Acknowledge their interest in your business and thank them for it.

Step 4: Answer a Question with a Question

Lead your prospect to the appointment or sale by using the porcupine technique. As you may recall, this refers to the scenario of throwing a porcupine in your lap – no doubt you would throw it right back! Use this technique for questioning over the phone. If your caller asks, "What if I don't have the time for a massage this week?" counter with, "Is the amount of time required for a full treatment a concern?" This gets the ball rolling and leads you directly to the heart of the real objection so you can overcome it.

Step 5: Reconfirm Details

Don't hang up until you've reconfirmed the details of your conversation, such as reiterating the day and time of an appointment. Ask your caller to grab a pen and write down your phone number in case she has questions later, then direct her to your website.

Additionally, when you talk to anyone on the phone, be sure that you are always courteous and do not lose your temper, no matter how frustrated or angry you may get.

Never leave a caller on hold for more than seventeen seconds. Any longer than that and your caller will have a bad attitude when you come back on the line. Always offer to call your prospect back if you must keep him on hold longer than seventeen seconds.

And if you work with others, make it a point to take good messages for them. Get a call back phone number, ask for the name and spell it properly and include the date and time of the call. How often have you gotten a message that was scribbled and tried to fake your way through it, "Uh...hello, Mrs. Wh...er...Wright. I see you called...today?" That's unprofessional. Train your employees to get the right information the first time and write it all down so someone else can read it!

Qualities of Successful Entrepreneurs

How do you get to be a successful entrepreneur? First, consider those qualities that define someone who wins more than loses, who knows how to handle each circumstance, and turn negatives into positives. What does that person look like? What does she do? How does she act?

The following traits have been compiled over many years and represent the most common qualities found in the most successful salespeople. Do your best to emulate them and you will find yourself attaining greater success that translates to a bigger bottom line.

Burning Desire to Achieve

Only you can measure if your desire to achieve is equal to the task at hand. Ask yourself, "How much pain can I handle until I quit?" and "How many problems can I put up with before throwing in the towel?" Your answers will determine just how much true desire you have.

If your desire is lacking, it could be you are focusing on the wrong goal. Go back to the goal setting exercises and review how to pare down your list to only those goals that you really want to or need to achieve.

Do What You Fear Most

A successful person learns what his fears are, attacks them one by one, then overcomes them. After this process, you will have the confidence necessary to do whatever it takes because you know your fears are groundless.

Constant Enthusiasm

Even when you fail, you must retain your sense of enthusiasm. Most people can't do this. Sure, it's easy to be enthusiastic at the beginning of a venture or when everything is going right, but you need to feel this way even when things are rough, and especially when things don't go as planned. When you've had a bad day, deal with it and look forward to the next day with positive passion. It comes back to the power of intention and the fact that you attract what you are. If you are enthusiastic about what you are offering, the people you present to will be, as well.

Love People

It is difficult, if not impossible, to use all the selling techniques presented here unless you truly love others. Remember that you are proud of what you do because you are helping someone overcome a problem. You can't look at prospects with dollar signs in your eyes; the other person will easily recognize this and resist your best efforts because they know you are not sincere. They need to see that you genuinely care about the people you serve; that is the balance that makes it all work.

Don't Take Rejection Personally

Remember that just because someone says, "No!" it doesn't mean they are rejecting you as a person. But...if this keeps happening, you need to seriously reconsider your sales presentation and identify what's not working.

Become a Student of Technique

Every great salesperson invests in his own education. You must believe that learning in the form of books, seminars, training sessions and more is a valuable resource to bolster your sales technique and your confidence.

Be open to learning. The more you educate yourself, the more apt you are to find a few golden nuggets that could really take your technique over the top. Sure, good training costs money but it's an investment in yourself. Aren't you worth it?

Practice Makes Perfect

It's not enough to simply sit in a seminar or read a book and soak up the information; you must put it into practice.

Try the S-P-R method for practicing your sales presentation:

- S – Stimulus
- P – Pause
- R – Response

The idea is to present a stimulant without pause and then expect a response. Animals never pause between a stimulant and their response; when your dog is hungry, he eats the food presented to him without any preamble. It's fine to add a pause when you are rehearsing, until you know your material well enough to not leave a break afterward. In this way you can capitalize on your prospect's natural response.

Practice, drill, rehearse – these are the three actions that will make a positive difference in your presentation. Practice, drill, and rehearse before you present it live! You need to know what to say and what to do before you interact with someone else. Think of being a sports professional, a tennis player perhaps. She's on the court with racquet in hand and the ball comes at her…does she have time to think about how to respond? No! She must respond instinctively, and that takes lots of practice. Learn proven responses to stimuli; know exactly what to answer before a question is asked. Learn your sales scripts inside and out, backward and forward.

Don't be like the average person who reacts to everything in life with the attitude, "I'll cross that bridge when I come to it." You must be prepared in order to find sales success that you can repeat over and over again, without conscious thought.

Creating Your Sales Presentation

Just as practice makes perfect, preplanning your sales presentation to accommodate everything you want to impart is very important. If you wish to build a house, you would work from a blueprint rather than just building upward or onward as you go without ensuring you have all the necessary materials. The same is necessary for a sales presentation that sells – you need to know what you are going to say in any scenario so you have the right material handy when you need it.

A good sales presentation revolves around outlining the benefits of your product or service. Remember, people buy benefits, not features. So you will want a list of benefits to use when making appointments via telephone, for qualifying prospects, and for demonstrating during an in-person presentation.

Anticipate the prospect's primary objection (we'll cover that more in the next chapter) and outline your responses in advance. It's a good idea to put this in writing so you can easily refer back to the list, add to it, or revise as necessary.

You must exhibit energy and enthusiasm during your presentation. Before you get started, take your vitamins; vitamins A, B, C, D and E:

- **A – Application**: Apply the things you have taught yourself.

- **B – Believability**: When people know you are telling the truth; they want to believe you. Make sure you use the right application and work on your believability to promote trust.

- **C – Comprehension**: Comprehend the emotions and feelings of the people to whom you are presenting. Stay cognizant of how your presentation is going by reviewing their faces frequently. Most consumers buy based on emotions and then justify the expenditure later. Learn how to strike while the iron is hot and get that final "Yes!" right at the table where your meeting is taking place.

- **D – Discipline**: Control what you do and focus on your ability to get it done. The amount of discipline you have is in direct proportion to your desire to succeed. Use that desire to exert your will over your natural propensity to procrastinate.

- **E – Enthusiasm**: You are only as good a presenter as your belief in the product or service you offer. You must be passionate about what you have to offer and believe that you can make a positive difference in the lives of others.

How often have you been in the middle of a sales presentation and found yourself losing control? In order to be successful, you must learn how to take control with questions. This is not to say that you must do all the talking. You have one mouth and a pair of ears so you can listen twice as much as you talk. Ask the right questions then patiently listen to the answers.

You can't tell your prospect that she needs something. That's being pushy and it's not well received. If you try to push the benefits of your product or service, it comes across as something positive for you more than for the prospect – and that doesn't close the sale.

Instead of telling, ask. Telling produces doubt; asking promotes belief. If you say it, they will doubt it. If they say it, they will believe it.

Tell yourself right now, "I won't tell my prospects things during my presentation. I will ask them."

This is important because your prospect needs to feel as if she alone made the buying decision. Your role is to ask a question she will answer in a way that makes her feel as if she made the decision, even though it was your influence that led her to the "right" answer. However, it's your obligation to make the decision for her.

How would you feel if you were lying on the operating table and your surgeon approached and said, "Here's the scalpel. Try it for a while." What if you made an appointment at your doctor's office and you crawled through the door, deathly ill, only to hear your doctor ask, "You look terrible! What do you think you have? I've got an extensive medical library; you may want to have a look." Your first job is to guide your clients' decisions; after all, that's why they came to you. You, as the professional, who knows the most about the products or services you are offering, must guide each client through the decision-making process, displaying confidence and knowledge.

There are many reasons why you must provide structure in your sales presentations through questioning:

- To gain control. With questions you lead the conversation; you are in absolute control.

- To isolate areas of interest so you can play them up and enjoy a better chance of getting the prospect to say yes.

- To acknowledge a fact. When you ask a question, the other person acknowledges it. You can then lead to the next level of closing.

- To receive a minor agreement by using the other person's interests.

- To arouse and control emotions. Remember that emotions arouse the purchase instinct.
- To isolate and answer objections. After you find out what the objections are, ask questions that allow the prospect to provide answers to his own objections.

So, can you learn how to sell? Look at your income right now. If you are not satisfied with what you are doing, or think you can do better, you have one of two options:

Learn the techniques of other successful people and model them

OR

Quit complaining and be happy with the life you are living.

Which one do you choose? Remember that all success starts with the decision to go after it. The process must first be cerebral and purposeful before your journey to success can be translated into the doing.

Chapter Eleven:
Handling Objection and Rejection

> *"An objection is not a rejection; it is simply a request for more information."*
> – Bo Bennett

Any time you are involved in selling a product or service, you will encounter objections to the sales process (but as you'll recall from the last chapter, you won't take it personally).

Have you ever heard someone complain, "Our Yellow Pages® ad isn't working – we aren't getting any clients from it!" or "Our marketing department isn't doing their job well enough because they aren't finding new clientele." They will use any excuse in the book for why they don't have new customers walking through the door – every excuse except laying the blame on themselves, where it truly belongs.

Selling is all about finding people to sell to and selling to the people you find. Until you figure out that formula, you will not find professional success.

Handling Objections

What about when you encounter objections from the people you are selling to – those excuses that your prospects are sure to come up with in order to resist the sale? How do you handle those objections?

Selling is like mental chess – it's a game that requires a lot of knowledge, thought, and preparation. Part of playing the game is anticipating your opponent's next move. While I don't advocate viewing sales as a competition pitting you against the prospect, the concept provides a powerful tool to help you determine how to respond to objections.

There are typically half a dozen common objections you will hear when selling any product or service. That is great news! That's not too many to prepare for and memorize the appropriate response.

You can choose to improve your objection handling techniques and responses by first identifying the most common ones in your industry; use this list to identify those you frequently encounter:

- I need to think about it.
- I don't have any money.
- I need to talk it over with someone.
- Can you fax me some information.
- I don't have the time.
- Your price is too high.

- I am already working with someone.
- We already tried it and it didn't work.
- I am not interested.

There are many ways to address these common objections. We will focus on a few of them here, which include:

- Story
- Non-stated objection
- Question
- Solve the problem
- Isolate
- Bring out the objection
- Script
- Investigate
- Before it comes up…
- Share the benefits
- Reduce the risk

- Negotiate

- What would need to happen?

Use a Story

One of the most powerful ways to handle an objection is responding with a story. "Reason why" stories are very persuasive because they act as invisible but powerful sales tools. Stories suspend time, so they take your prospect to a different situation where they can imagine a better life and better circumstances.

Start by identifying true stories that address each objection. Learn them and memorize them so it becomes second nature to relate them to your prospect.

Here's an example. Let's say you offer a health product and you've found the most common objection is its cost. Ask your prospect if there is anything else preventing him from buying your product. Address that objection with a story that might start like this, "Your fear of spending too much reminds me of a story about a client who was in a similar situation. Let me share with you what he did." You might go on to relate a story about a man who let a debilitating health problem go until he could no longer do his job. He waited too long before realizing how important his health was to his family and his livelihood. After buying your product, he was able to go back to work and…you get the idea. The story will make a powerful impression on your prospects because it's something they can relate to.

Non-Stated Objections

Often times the true objection is a non-stated objection. The prospect might tell you why he won't buy, but this reason isn't the real one. In this case you must become the Objection Detective, asking questions to figure out what's really at the root of the prospect's resistance.

Question

Objections are easily countered by answering them with a question. This puts the ball back in the other person's court and helps them work through the reason their objection really isn't valid.

For example:
- Objection: "The price is too high."
  - Possible responses:
    - "By too high what exactly do you mean?"
    - "How much is the price too high?"
    - "Compared to what?"

- Objection: "I don't have the time."
  - Possible responses:
    - "When will you have the time?"
    - "On a scale of one to ten, how motivated are you to move forward?"
    - "What do you mean by that?"

You can see how these questioning responses open up a dialogue instead of leaving the sale on the table. Questions require responses and the majority of people simply can't leave them unanswered.

Solve the Problem

One way to handle an objection is to solve the problem it presents, taking away the prospect's reason for not performing the action you desire.

Let's look at an example. If you were in the network marketing business you might invite a prospect to a meeting at a local hotel on a Wednesday night. The prospect might say she can't get a babysitter that night. You could solve the problem by offering to have your sister babysit. Maybe she doesn't have a ride; then you offer to drive her. In any case, your goal is to solve the problem and make the objection invalid.

Isolate

Isolating the objection is one of my favorite techniques. I like it because it is very effective and easy to learn. Here is an example:

- Objection: "I don't have the money."
    - Response: "I can appreciate that. Other than the money involved, is there anything else preventing you from taking action today?" In this case, you are asking a closing question; be silent afterward as you wait for a response.

- Objection: "I don't have the time."
  - Response: "Other than the time required, is there anything else preventing you from moving forward today?"

You can see how these questions help you delve deeper into the prospect's true objection. Once you know the real problem, you can address it using the preplanned script your created based on the most common objections you encounter.

Script

We've already talked about sales scripts in general, but dealing with objections is another instance when it pays to have a pre-planned script.

- Objection: "I need to speak with my wife first."
  - Response: "I understand this is an important decision and you wish to discuss it with your wife. If your

wife agrees that this is a fantastic opportunity, does that mean you will sign the contract?" This is a trial close.

Wait for a positive response, then ask, "What if she doesn't agree?" This is another trial close where you are asking for a commitment.

Be silent as you wait for the answer so your prospect feels the need to step in and speak. This increases your chance of receiving a positive response.

Investigate

Sometimes you need to be a detective in getting to the real heart of the prospect's objection. This happens when the prospect isn't so eager to share information. In this case, you can try, "Tell me more about that" in an attempt to get him to open up.

Before It Comes Up

This is one of the most powerful objection handling techniques. You can reverse engineer your sales presentation to anticipate the objections the prospect might offer, based on your past sales experience. You will address any possible objections in the body of your sales presentation, right up front.

One of my clients sells $6,000 wealth building seminars. An objection he often encounters is, "I am already a millionaire. What do I need your program for?"

How does he handle the objection? By pre-planning for it! It is in his script to ask the prospect, "I am sure you are familiar with Donald Trump. Is that true?" He then waits for a positive response and asks, "Would you agree that he is a great businessman?" Once again, he waits for the positive response. "After Trump became a multimillionaire he made some bad financial decisions. In fact he lost so much money he went upside down $900 million. One day Trump was walking in downtown Manhattan with his then wife, Marla Maples. He said, 'Marla, you see that bum right there? He is worth $900 million more than I am.' Although Trump is a great businessman, he made some huge mistakes when it came to wealth building. If Trump was a client of ours we could have helped prevent the loss of his wealth. It is great that you have a net worth in the millions right now. We help clients like you not only increase your wealth, but also preserve it. Some of our top clients are multimillionaires like yourself."

Do you see how smoothly that objection was handled? This technique works for my client nine times out of ten....

How to Handle Failure and Rejection

I'm going to let you in on one more secret to success: see at least ten to twenty people per day. Yep, that's all it takes – personal meetings with at least ten to twenty people each and every workday. You need to have belly-to-belly meetings where you interact with someone in person, not phone appointments and not email interaction. The more people you actually see, the more money you will make.

Unfortunately, many entrepreneurs refuse to believe this. And there's only one reason they fight tooth and nail against talking to more people who could be converted from prospect to paying client – fear. It's a fear of rejection.

Think back to when you were just a baby. What's the first word you were taught? It was "no". Your parents taught you that word because they loved you and didn't want anything to harm you. As an adult, the only word standing between who you are right now and who you want to become is the word "no".

Don't fear rejection, embrace it. After you've been rejected, go out and find one more lead. Why? Because you want to end your day on a positive note. Your attitude is one of the most important parts of the sales equation and in order to maintain a positive attitude, you need to taste success by closing one more customer before calling it quits.

There is a formula to keep in mind when you think about possible rejection from one more person: One sale = $100. If you contact ten people (using the ratio of ten leads = one sale), then one out of those ten will say yes; nine will say no. At this point you've earned $100 and the value of each "no" is $10.

Now use this formula to change your attitude about rejection. When you see ten people and make one sale worth $100, it cost you $10 per person – a mere pittance, right! That's a positive way of looking at the rejection you faced from those nine other people.

This is a concept you can use in your personal life as well as your professional life. It will help you cope with rejection from anyone, face failure, and stay positive. Each rejection costs a tiny amount, not enough to miss.

I never view rejection as failure or failure as rejection. Instead, I consider it a learning experience. Consider Thomas Edison. He was once asked by an interviewer how he felt about failing a thousand times before finally discovering how to make a working light bulb. His response? "I didn't fail; I only learned a thousand ways it didn't work." Now that's a great attitude!

Think of failure as negative feedback – the feedback you need to change your course to find success. We all make mistakes; isn't it great that someone, at some point, will identify them so you can correct them and move on?

I want you to learn these four phrases and memorize them. Keep them in mind every time you feel frustrated or fearful of failure:

- "I never see failure as failure but only the negative feedback I need to change course in my direction."
- "I never see failure as failure but only as the opportunity to develop my sense of humor."
- "I never see failure as failure but only as the opportunity to practice my techniques and perfect my performance."
- "I never see failure as failure but only as the game I must play to win."

Emotions: Sales Triggers

Seldom do people buy products using logic. People buy with their emotions, then defend the sale logically afterward.

Think of the various emotions people might use to justify their purchase. They may include:

- Regaining health
- Better quality of life
- To look and feel better
- To enjoy the latest fashion or style
- Pride of ownership
- Security
- Peer pressure
- Self-improvement

Think about the advertising you see on television. When you buy products at the grocery store, chances are you are using the emotions triggered by the advertisements you have seen, even if you haven't consciously absorbed the message. For instance, you may choose a specific peanut butter because of an ad that makes you feel you are only a good mother when you select a certain brand. Even toilet paper ads work on your emotions by making you believe that one brand is softer and cuddlier than the other.

Emotions can trigger a sale, but they can also destroy a sale. If your manner is too pushy, you create an emotion of fear and prospects will begin to fight you in order to overcome that fear. Remember that you fear rejection and that's why you may not be as successful as you could be. The person you are selling to feels fear, too. Turn that negative emotion into a positive one so the prospect feels good about buying.

If you begin the sales process using the wrong words, that triggers fear – and rejection. Rejection words are any words or phrases that incite fear or let prospects consciously know you are trying to sell something. Some of the most common rejection words used in a selling situation and a more positive way to reword those terms are:

- **Commission**: Instead use "fee" or "fee for service", as in "The service you will receive over the years will far outweigh any fee you have paid."

- **Cost or Price**: The prospect will think, "I'll shop for a better one." Instead, use the term "total investment".

- **Down payment**: Instead use "initial investment".

- **Monthly payment**: Replace this with "monthly investment" or "total amount".

- **Contract**: Say "paperwork" or refer to "the agreement".

- **Buy**: Replace this word with "own", as in "When you own this lovely car…"
- **Sell or Sold**: Use the term "involved" as in, "I got Jim involved in this tax program". People would much rather be involved than sold.
- **Deal**: Use "opportunity" as in, "I have an excellent opportunity for you."
- **Sign**: This word makes people anxious; instead ask them to "okay" or "approve" the forms, "authorize" or "autograph" the contract, as in "Let me make you famous and have you autograph this."
- **Pitch**: This makes it sound as if what you are saying isn't true; replace this word with "presentation", "Thanks for giving me an opportunity to show you my presentation."

- **Problem**: Refer to this is as a "challenge" instead, as in "We've faced that challenge before" or "We can help you overcome that challenge."
- **Objection**: Instead use "area of concern" as in, "I can appreciate that area of concern."
- **Cheaper**: this word demeans the value of your product or service so use "more economical" or "less expensive".
- **Prospects**: Refer to them in person as "future clients".
- **Back Ordered**: This can be referred to as a "fortunate oversell situation" – learn to make it positive by alluding to the fact that your product is so popular you can't keep up with demand!

Are you ready to face your next challenge and overcome mistakes, rather than face failure and view it as rejection? The time to put these concepts into practice is now.

Chapter Twelve:
Lead Like You Want to be Lead

> *"Leadership is the art of getting someone else to do something you want done because he wants to do it."*
> – Dwight D. Eisenhower
>
> *"Treat people as if they were what they ought to be and you help them become what they are capable of becoming."* – Johan Goethe

How effective are you at working in a team? This is a skill vital to effective management of any company, however large or small.

When you start a business of your own you will be alone, at least at the very beginning. There will be no one to tell you what to do, nobody to motivate and support you. You must take responsibility for yourself and to a certain degree, for any possible partners such as suppliers, family members, and even customers who support your venture both in front of and behind the scenes.

No one can work alone all the time. At some point you will need to add members to your team in order to grow your business. Working with others, instead of trying to be everything and do it all yourself, is the way you can accomplish more and improve your bottom line – and isn't that one of your goals?

It's one thing to be a good entrepreneur, it's another thing altogether to realize the greater value of being part of an effective team. As a business owner it is your job to head a group of talented people and lead them to success for all. It is also your job to not only help them survive but thrive. You will be the glue that holds them all together, the leading force that fills in the blank spots created by your weaknesses.

You need the right people for the right jobs. That means you must make an honest assessment of who you are and what you've got right now so that you may identify the missing pieces.

Working in a team you get much more accomplished than you ever could as a solo artist. Sure, it's your commitment and motivation that started your business, but it also required a little help from your friends (and family and customers and everyone else who is part of the supply and demand chain). If you feel you really don't need anyone else in your business venture, then chances are your goals are simply too small.

The more you take on team members for the right reason – to help them – the more you will be rewarded with trustworthy, knowledgeable, and loyal employees and suppliers who learn the skills necessary to make your business an unequivocal success. It's up to you to identify the holes in your business and then fill them with people you admire and trust.

Investing In Your Team

When your goal is to build a strong team that works together for everyone's good, you must be willing to make an investment in those human resources. The members of your team are like links in the big chain of your business. If one of them breaks, the whole thing falls apart. When all are strong, because everyone is contributing to the best of their ability, the odds of success for all become much greater.

Developing a team with a great work ethic requires continual teaching and training. Just as the successful entrepreneur must be coachable, she should also be willing to make an investment of both time and money in the team members she relies on.

I'm not just talking about sending your employees or other support personnel to training sessions and conferences. It takes a personal commitment to ensure that you take care of your team like you would your family members. In fact, the work environment should be modeled on a family environment. It should be like a second home; a happy place that people truly want to be.

In my own business, I plan annual get-togethers and invite everyone who works in my clinics, along with their family members. I always host a barbecue in a location outside of work where the goal is for everyone to have fun and share with each other personally. That helps us get to know each other better and really care about helping one another achieve success.

It's important that every team member have an attitude of helping and encouraging each other. My team provides both support and encouragement in genuine doses and as the leader, I set the example for others to follow.

As long as my employees care about making and achieving goals – whether personal or professional – I care about them, too, and do whatever is necessary to support them. That means I dig deep into my own pockets to help them financially as well as providing an ear when they need to talk things out. I allow them to grow, to spread their wings and reach for the stars. Because of this, I am able to attract quality personnel. That also translates to better sales; when clients walk into my clinics they feel a cozy family atmosphere and respond positively to the genuine warmth and love there.

At one point in my career I decided to buy into a franchise business. It ended up falling flat and I actually lost a great deal of money. However, the failure of my franchise taught me many valuable lessons. One of those lessons was how to treat people as treasured, indispensable parts of my business – the links in a chain. Even after leaving the franchise, many of my former team members called and asked if there were any future opportunities to be in my circle again. That's how closely knit we became and how much value they received from working for me.

Of course, I can't take care of everything on my own. I have leaders within my company whom I've trained to take over managerial tasks when I am not available. A business can't become sustainable without outside leadership; team management is more powerful than individual management. Train your leaders to train their employees and you will create a strong team able to accomplish anything!

Creating Trust

Building a strong team requires one key ingredient: trust. You can't train managers and employees then allow them the freedom to fail unless you completely trust that they have your best interests at heart.

Many entrepreneurs feel that trusting others to make important decisions makes them weak. They feel the need to be at their businesses every single day, overseeing operations and ensuring they maintain complete control. That is a recipe for disaster! You must give up at least some of your control so that your business may benefit from the input of others with unique talents, knowledge and experience. Trust must be earned, but it can't be earned until you first learn to relinquish control.

Remember that we reviewed how successful people are bound to fail but instead of allowing that experience to be an excuse to quit, they use it as a way to free themselves from the fear of failure. The same is true of your team; you must allow them to fail forward rather than fall backward and quit. That's not easy, particularly when you see the results of all your hard work in jeopardy. But unless you give your employees a blank checkbook, how much do you truly have to lose? Chances are it's much less than you can imagine in a worst case scenario.

Trust is the key to creating a self-sustaining business. You will never be able to go on vacation and truly let go of business concerns unless you know you've got a great team working just as hard at your business as they would at their own.

Those who first worked with me in my clinics became some of the most loyal and trustworthy employees with whom I've ever had the pleasure of working. They are still with me today and I rest easy knowing I can call them any time, day or night, and they will drop anything to help me out. That's the power of trust, an essential ingredient in any great organization. It's also a wonderful fail safe for those times when you need a bit of help in a hurry.

Traits of a Successful Team Leader

Successful entrepreneurs are team leaders who know when to delegate tasks based on their time constraints and weaknesses. But...you can only lead others if you have your own fears under control and are willing to take risks. You cannot be afraid of doing what needs to be done and thus setting a good example for your team. You must take risks without fear of failure so you can promote this trait in your team members – and allow them to fail forward with confidence. Those are just two essentials traits of every great team leader. Here are a few more.

Personal Integrity

You cannot expect someone else in your organization to act with strong convictions, standards and morals unless you embody those traits. You must have personal integrity that is clearly shown in every action you take in order to expect the same from those in your employ. And when you act in a way that undoubtedly demonstrates your integrity, you gain the trust of your team.

Professional integrity means you live by a Code of Honor. You must be honest with your customers and suppliers and never mislead them. We've looked at various ways you can close a deal but none of them rely on deception or doing something that would be against the best interests of the other party.

How you do anything is how you do everything – is your course set true to your moral compass by acting with integrity in all business dealings? Thomas Jefferson once said, "In matters of style, swim with the current; in matters of principle, stand like a rock." You must be the rock your team relies upon and uses for a shining example of doing what's right in any circumstance.

Share a Clear Vision

How can you lead your team to success if you don't know where your business is headed? And how can you expect your team to go along on the journey unless you share the destination?

As you know, successful entrepreneurs use plans and goals to achieve success. But too often those plans and goals aren't shared with the team responsible for making it all happen. Too often they are either left to figure it out themselves or given goals and deadlines without the big picture in place. Neither of those scenarios are effective in taking your organization and your team to the next level.

Visualize the future. Set your goals based on that vision. Share it with everyone who has the ability to support it. Then help your team turn that vision into reality, with specific goals and actions they will be motivated to complete.

Positive Enthusiasm

Many entrepreneurs lament a lack of motivated employees. They complain that their team members put in minimal effort and exhibit little excitement at the thought of reaching the organization's goals.

If that is you, take a step back and review your leadership performance. Do you exhibit enthusiasm while discussing your vision for the business? If you can't get excited about setting and making goals, you can't expect your employees to be motivated by them, either. It's up to you to set the example by showing positive enthusiasm in everything you do – even if it's a small task like cleaning the restrooms!

Creative Problem Solving

If there is a problem in your business, it's up to you to fix it. Yes, you have a great team that supports your efforts, but in the end it's your job to be the problem solver, to be a real leader.

That doesn't mean you can't ask for your team's input in deciding how to handle problems; in fact, it's a good idea to do so. Promote creativity by asking your employees and managers to think about all possible solutions, no matter how wild and crazy they may at first seem. Then go through the list as a team and decide which course of action is best. You might be surprised at the creative solutions you entertain when you ask for the input of those intimately involved in your business.

This also shows your employees how much you trust them and that you value their opinions. This provides deeper meaning for their work which, in turn, promotes motivation. Your team members want to know their voices are being heard. They will feel empowered and view themselves as vital components in the formula of success.

Action Catalyst

By now you realize that no success is possible without action. I've been to many corporate meetings where everyone gathered around a big table and discussed goals, problems and initiatives but at the end of the meeting, everyone just stood up and walked out the door. No one decided to take action on the items discussed, and no goals were set!

Does that sound like your company? If so, it's important that you become the catalyst for action; motivate your employees to do whatever needs to be done, no matter how seemingly insignificant, boring or even frightening. Remember that you must lead by example, so show them that you are willing to do no less than what you ask of others.

Get your team up and moving about, physically, so they become energized to do the tasks necessary to take your business where it needs to go. It goes without saying that you must develop a subset of goals, assign human resources to complete them and designate deadlines – then reward your employees when they achieve success.

But nothing is going to happen until you become the catalyst for action. Start the process by being a good example.

Challenge Your Team to Over-Achieve

Have you ever heard of the "Pygmalion Effect"? This refers to nothing more than expecting others to live up to a higher expectation. You may have some overachievers hidden in your organization who merely need to be challenged in order to perform at their maximum capabilities.

What will happen if you expect more than an employee has shown? For one, you are creating a challenge and people love rising to a challenge. For another, you are promoting self-growth and raising self-esteem when the obstacle is overcome. Most people love to stretch their wings and try something they've never done before; when they find success, they experience euphoria and are ready to be challenged to meet the next, even higher goal. This provides self-motivation on the job that you cannot equal with any other method, even the promise of more money!

The key here is not to go overboard. Don't expect the mailroom clerk to make a $1 million sale tomorrow. But do expect him to be able to answer some of your correspondence, and perhaps even make appointments based on the communication coming into the mailroom.

Promote Excellence

While you always want your team members to achieve each and every goal, you must be aware that won't always be the case. You can set lofty goals but expect that some simply won't be met, not due to indifference or lack of motivation, but merely because we are all humans and none of us are perfect.

You can't expect perfection, but you can expect excellence. Once again, you must lead by example. Exhibit excellence in everything you do, no matter how small, and insist on the same from your team. You cannot tolerate anything less than an individual's best efforts.

When you have a team member who is struggling to produce quality results, it could be that she is missing the knowledge or training needed. That's when a true leader takes the time to mentor and coach, providing the employee with the necessary training to develop the right skills to do the job properly. You may also want to form a team of the underperforming employee and a manager or someone else who knows his job exceptionally well. Let the two of them work together to identify areas that need work and come up with appropriate solutions.

Once you've given your underperforming team member the proper environment and knowledge, do not accept anything less than the excellence you know is possible.

Nurture Relationships

If you've ever felt you must take on the role of a parent to your employees, you are probably not far from the truth. In fact, an effective team leader knows how to nurture relationships so members grow as closely knit as a family.

It's important for team members to feel they are loved. Showing that you care about others does not make you a weak or ineffective leader; in fact Kahlil Gibran is noted for saying that "Tenderness and kindness are not signs of weakness and despair, but manifestations of strength and resolutions." True leadership benefits your employees by making them part of an exclusive, inner circle focused on the success not only of your organization, but of its members. It is up to you to create an environment where everyone feels safe, secure and valued.

Of course, as it is with any relationship, people aren't always going to get along or see eye to eye. You must mediate disputes (or at least assign a manager to do so) and ensure that each person feels his voice is being heard. Your employees don't need to be best friends – and it's probably better that they aren't – but they do need to feel that their differences are acceptable and perhaps even celebrated.

Confidence and Certainty

The timid entrepreneur is not a good leader. It takes courage, but you must show your team members that you are confident in moving toward the goals you've set. This is based on the data available; if you have a lot of information on which to base your decision, you will enjoy a high level of certainty. Conversely, if you are lacking information, your certainty level will be low. In either case, it's up to you, as the business owner, to lead your team toward success by making a decision that you expect everyone to support.

If you have low information and low certainty, it may be time to rethink your plan. Feeling that you do not have the resources, time, skills, knowledge or money available to execute a plan confuses your employees, who will lack the necessary motivation and commitment to attain the goal. Sometimes it's better to scrap an idea rather than risk damaging the self-esteem of your employees.

Find the personal meaning and strength in each decision, then lead your team with confidence and certainty. Remember that if you are optimistic about the odds of reaching your goals (and you should be via the power of intention), that will translate positively to your team and help them realize that anything is possible.

Transform Strengths Into Talents

A diverse team is one that can combine the talents of its members into a strong, unified force with which to be reckoned. A great team leader will identify those talents, and turn them into strengths.

Trust once again plays a part in this trait; you must trust that you have selected the right people for the job and that they have the abilities to get the job done without fail.

It also goes back to your ability as team leader to expect more from each of your employees. Expect that each one can use their God-given talents to accomplish what needs to be done. Expect excellence.

Nurture employees by giving them positive feedback and encouraging them to set the bar higher and higher each time they achieve a goal. Coach them so that their passions translate into positive action for the organization. This is how you can turn a talent into a strength and an average employee into a dependable, committed, self-motivated, integral part of your team.

In any kind of business, you are sure to be surrounded at some point by hostile forces. Wouldn't you rather find yourself in the midst of a loving, caring team than adrift on the ocean in a single-person canoe?

Chapter Thirteen:
The Sum of Everything Within

> *"What lies behind us and what lies ahead of us are tiny matters compared to what lives within us."* – Henry David Thoreau

This book provides a lot of information. It might seem overwhelming to review and commit that information to memory. It may seem impossible to use all the ways you've learned to reset your mind to find success.

Rather than be tempted to take no action because the task of achieving success seems too daunting, remember that you can break down your large goal into smaller chunks. Rather than set a goal of "I want to be more successful" drill down on that broad statement and break it up into more manageable chunks. Start with one personal and one professional goal, then use the techniques you've learned to create a plan with doable action steps.

By now you should also realize that we are our own biggest supporters *and* worst enemies. We can simply decide to do nothing because that's the easy route. But remember that you will never be completely comfortable doing everything to succeed. That's okay. You know you have the inner strength and you can draw on that anytime. Don't forget that the power of intention is on your side, as well as the members of your team. Success requires support. It's not a sign of weakness to ask for help; it takes a strong, confident person to admit when they need the talents, skills and knowledge of others. In fact, that's the big reason I decided to write this book; after years of being a student of successful people, I wanted to put all that information in one place in order to help others, just like you, emulate their success.

Achieving goals is intentional. Most people believe they should be successful and have goals, but rarely do they turn dreams into action. They allow their subconscious to dictate the course of their lives. They never bring their minds onboard with their goals; never ask the universe to provide the awesome power of intention to bring about the correct circumstances at the proper time.

Only you are in control of your destiny. It is up to you to examine your belief system, and throw out the false information and fears that hold you back from success. It is up to you to replace a negative mindset with positive thoughts and fill yourself only with positive, good, affirming information. Remember that your comfort zone is a self-erected barrier to success and focus on the actions you can take each and every day as a part of your personal routine in order to blast through that barrier.

Of course you dreams won't get any farther than your head until you set goals for yourself. Take the goals you've put in writing and place them somewhere you will see them every day; many people tape the list onto their bathroom mirror so it's the first thing they see each morning and the last thing they view before going to bed each night. That's also a great place to post a note that includes your big "why" in bold letters and colors. Whenever your motivation flags, look at that note and remind yourself why you are doing what you are doing. Many people will give up right before they reach success; don't let your efforts be wasted because you lost motivation or commitment.

Quit spending time listening to your little voice (is it chiming in right about now, telling you can't do this?) and spend more time on the things you've prioritized as highest on your list of to-dos.

Control that little voice in your head. Ensure that you examine what's working right now and what areas you need to change. Devise scripts that deal with each sales scenario you experience in your line of work. Keep them handy and refer to them so often that you've got them memorized. There's no point wasting time trying to reinvent what you say to prospects or clients in the future when you already know what works – use it to sell, sell, sell and make more money each and every day! Even if financial security isn't a high priority goal for you at this time, growing your business with a proven system is a way for you to change the other areas of your life that need some help.

Above all, remember to do all things for love and with love. The power of the universe will work for you as long as you have the right intentions. Lift yourself up and do the same for others. Not only do you need and deserve support, encouragement, kindness and caring but so do others in your life. Do your best for others and you will find the best in your own life.

Mindset and action are equal partners in your journey to success. You have the tools and the know-how and the motivation to become more than the majority of those who will start goals but never complete them. That is the biggest reason why people fail and I know you will not fail because you have the recipe for success.

Now get out there and DO! I'm confident you will find success and start living the life you truly deserve!

7

Made in the USA
Charleston, SC
23 October 2012